# Perplexity: The Research Playbook

AI-Powered Search and Research for Everyone

Ken Tannenbaum

**2026**

Finnoybu Press

# Perplexity: The Research Playbook

## 2026 Edition

### AI-Powered Search and Research for Everyone

---

**Published by Finnoybu Press**



For permissions and inquiries: press@finnoybu.org



**First Edition:** 2026

## About the Author

**Ken Tannenbaum** is a technologist, entrepreneur, and AI governance researcher. He is the founder of Finnoybu Press and the founder/steward of the AEGIS Initiative, an open framework for AI safety and accountability. Learn more at aegis-initiative.com.

When he's not building governance standards for artificial intelligence, he's helping everyday people understand and use it.

## Dedication

For everyone who has ever typed a question into a search bar and thought, “There has to be a better way to find this.”

There is. You are holding it.

## The AI for Everyone Series

---

This book is part of the **AI for Everyone** series by Finnoybu Press, designed to help real people use AI tools effectively. Visit **press.finnoybu.org** for the latest titles and updates.

### Collection One: Product Deep Dives

- *ChatGPT: The Definitive Guide (2026 Edition)*
- *ChatGPT: The Power User Guide (2026 Edition)*
- *Claude: The Definitive Guide (2026 Edition)*
- *Claude Code: The Power User Guide (2026 Edition)*
- *Gemini: The Complete Guide (2026 Edition)*
- *Gemini: The Advanced Guide (2026 Edition)*
- *Copilot: The Workplace AI Guide (2026 Edition)*
- *Copilot: The Advanced Workplace Guide (2026 Edition)*
- *Perplexity: The Research Playbook (2026 Edition)*
- *Perplexity: The Advanced Research Playbook (2026 Edition)*

### Collection Two: Product Guides

- *NotebookLM: From Sources to Audio Overviews (2026 Edition)*
- *DeepSeek: Code, Math, and Reasoning (2026 Edition)*
- *Cursor: The AI Code Editor (2026 Edition)*
- *OpenClaw: Agentic AI for Everyday Work (2026 Edition)*

### Collection Three: Cross-Platform Skills

- *AI Systems Playbook (2026 Edition)*
- *AI Prompt Engineering (2026 Edition)*
- *AI for Developers (2026 Edition)*
- *AI for Business (2026 Edition)*
- *AI for Students (2026 Edition)*
- *AI Governance for Practitioners (2026 Edition)*
- *Securing Agentic AI (2026 Edition)*

# Table of Contents

# Introduction

## What This Book Is About

This book teaches you how to use Perplexity AI — the search tool that reads the web so you do not have to. By the time you finish, you will know how to get clear, cited answers to any question, conduct serious research using Deep Research and Spaces, choose the right AI model for different tasks, and integrate Perplexity into your daily workflow for school, work, or curiosity.

We start at the beginning — what Perplexity is, how to set it up, and how to run your first search — and work through every major feature the platform offers in 2026. No prior experience with AI tools is required. If you can use a search engine, you can use this book.

## Who This Book Is For

You are in the right place if any of the following describe you:

- You have heard about Perplexity and want to know what it does and whether it is worth your time
- You have tried Perplexity casually but suspect you are scratching the surface
- You are a student, professional, or researcher looking for better ways to find and synthesize information
- You are evaluating AI search tools and want an honest assessment of what Perplexity can and cannot do

This book assumes no technical background. You do not need to understand how AI models work to use Perplexity effectively, though we will explain the basics where it helps you make better decisions.

## The Companion Book

This is the beginner's guide. It covers everything you need to go from zero to confident, productive use. If you want to push further — advanced prompting strategies, API development, enterprise deployment, and power-user workflows

— the companion volume, *Perplexity: The Advanced Research Playbook (2026 Edition)*, picks up where this book leaves off.

## How to Read This Book

The chapters are organized in a logical progression, and first-time readers will benefit from reading them in order. That said, each chapter stands on its own, so if you already know the basics and want to jump straight to Deep Research (Chapter 12) or Spaces (Chapter 10), go ahead.

The book is divided into five parts. Part I covers orientation and setup. Part II introduces the core features you will use every day. Part III goes deep on the platform's advanced capabilities. Part IV addresses specific audiences and use cases. Part V covers critical thinking, ethics, and what to watch for when relying on AI-powered search.

Practical exercises appear throughout. Do them. Reading about Perplexity teaches you concepts; using Perplexity builds skill.

## AI Disclosure

This book was written with the assistance of AI tools. All content was reviewed, revised, and approved by the author. The analysis, opinions, and recommendations are the author's own.

## A Note About Accuracy

Perplexity changes constantly. The company ships updates regularly, sometimes weekly. Features get added, interfaces get redesigned, models get upgraded. This book is accurate as of May 2026, but specific details — menu locations, exact pricing, feature availability — may have shifted by the time you read this.

The principles, techniques, and strategies in this book have a much longer shelf life than the interface details. How to ask better questions, evaluate sources, and structure research with Spaces and Deep Research — those skills transfer across versions and even across different AI tools.

When something seems different from what's described here, check Perplexity's help center at perplexity.ai/help for the latest information.

## Let's Get Started

Open Perplexity on whatever device is closest to you. You will want it handy as you read. The best way to learn a tool is to use it while someone explains it – and that is what we are about to do.

# Part I: Getting Started

*"The important thing is not to stop questioning. Curiosity has its own reason for existing."*

— Albert Einstein

# Chapter 1: What Is Perplexity AI?

## The Search Engine That Actually Answers Your Questions

You have had this experience a thousand times. You type a question into a search engine, hit enter, and get back a wall of blue links. You click the first one. It is a listicle stuffed with ads. You go back, try the second link. It is behind a paywall. The third loads slowly and does not quite answer what you asked. Twenty minutes later, you have opened eight tabs, skimmed four articles, and pieced together a rough answer you are only somewhat confident about.

Perplexity AI was built to eliminate that ritual.

Instead of handing you a list of websites and wishing you luck, Perplexity reads the web for you, synthesizes what it finds, and delivers a direct, sourced answer. Every claim comes with a citation you can click to verify. It is not a chatbot pretending to know things. It is not a search engine hoping you will figure it out. The company calls it an "answer engine," and once you use it, you will see why that distinction matters.

## How Perplexity Works — The Short Version

At its core, Perplexity combines two technologies that are powerful on their own but transformative together: large language models and real-time web search.

**Large language models** — the same technology behind tools like ChatGPT and Claude — are AI systems trained on enormous amounts of text. They are good at understanding questions, reasoning through problems, and generating clear, natural-language responses. Their weakness is that their training data has a cutoff date. Ask a standalone LLM about something that happened last week, and it will either confess ignorance or, worse, confidently make something up.

**Real-time web search** solves that problem. When you ask Perplexity a question, it does not rely solely on what a model was trained on months ago. It goes out to the live web, finds relevant current sources, and feeds that information to the language model. The model then synthesizes everything into a coherent answer and attaches citations so you can see where each piece came from.

The combination gives you the conversational clarity of an AI assistant with the factual grounding of a search engine. Answers are current, sourced, and written in plain language — not ten blue links and a prayer.

## What Makes Perplexity Different from Google

If Perplexity is a search tool and Google is a search tool, why would you switch? The difference runs deeper than it first appears.

**Google is a directory.** When you search Google, you are asking it to point you toward web pages that might contain your answer. Google is extraordinarily good at this — it indexes an almost incomprehensible amount of the web and uses sophisticated algorithms to rank results. But the work of reading, evaluating, and synthesizing still falls on you. Google finds the haystack; you locate the needle.

**Perplexity is a researcher.** When you ask Perplexity a question, it does the reading for you. It pulls from multiple sources, cross-references information, and presents a unified answer. You do not need to open tabs, skim articles, or mentally merge conflicting accounts from different websites. Perplexity handles that cognitive labor and shows its work through citations.

This does not mean Google is obsolete — far from it. If you want to navigate to a specific website, find a local restaurant, or browse shopping results, Google remains excellent. But for the kind of search where you want an answer to a question — "What are the health effects of intermittent fasting?" or "How does ranked-choice voting work?" or "What happened at the Fed meeting yesterday?" — Perplexity is often faster and more useful.

## What Makes Perplexity Different from ChatGPT and Claude

A question comes up constantly: if Perplexity uses language models, how is it different from just asking ChatGPT or Claude directly?

The critical difference is **citations and real-time web access by default**.

When you ask ChatGPT or Claude a question, you are primarily drawing on the model's training data. These systems have added web search over time, but it is not always on, and the integration varies. More importantly, their responses typically do not provide granular, inline citations for every factual claim.

Perplexity was designed from the ground up as a search-first tool. Every response is grounded in live web sources. Every factual statement links back to where it came from. You never have to wonder, "Is the AI making this up?" because you can click the citation and check.

Think of it this way: ChatGPT and Claude are brilliant conversationalists who sometimes look things up. Perplexity is a researcher who happens to communicate in natural language. Both are valuable, but they serve different needs.

## A Brief History of Perplexity AI

Perplexity was founded by Aravind Srinivas, a former researcher at Google and DeepMind — two of the most influential AI research organizations in the world. The company launched with a clear thesis: the way people search for information online is broken, and AI can fix it.

That thesis resonated. Perplexity grew rapidly, attracting millions of users tired of the traditional search experience. By 2026, the platform has surpassed 34 million monthly active users and a valuation of approximately 20 billion dollars. Those are not just impressive numbers for an AI startup — they signal that a lot of people have found lasting value in a different way of searching.

In February 2026, the company made a notable strategic decision: abandon advertising entirely and commit to a subscription-only business model. In an era when nearly every free internet service is funded by ads — and the perverse incentives that come with them — Perplexity chose to align its revenue directly with user satisfaction. If the tool is not useful enough to pay for, the company does not make money. That alignment matters, and we will explore the plan options in Chapter 2.

## What Perplexity Can Do

Before we get into plans, setup, and advanced features in later chapters, here is a high-level tour of what Perplexity offers in 2026. Think of this as a map of the territory we will explore together.

### Answer Questions with Citations

This is the foundation. Ask any question — factual, analytical, creative, technical — and get a clear answer with sources. Simple, but the execution is what makes it special.

### Pro Search

For complex questions that need deeper investigation, Pro Search performs multi-step reasoning. Instead of doing a single search and summarizing the results, it breaks your question into sub-queries, searches multiple times, evaluates what it finds, and synthesizes a more thorough answer. It is the difference between a quick glance and real research.

### Focus Modes

Perplexity lets you direct your searches toward specific types of content. Want only academic papers? There is a mode for that. Only videos? Financial data? Reddit discussions? Focus modes narrow the scope of your search to the kind of information you want.

### Deep Research

When you need a comprehensive investigation — not just an answer but a full report — Deep Research goes far beyond what a standard search provides. It can generate detailed reports, presentations, and dashboards on complex topics. Think of it as a research assistant who works in minutes instead of hours.

### Spaces

Spaces are collaborative environments where you can organize research around a project or topic. If you are working on a thesis, planning a trip, or researching a business decision, a Space keeps all your related searches, notes, and findings in one place.

### Pages

Perplexity can transform your research into polished, publishable web pages. Once you have gathered information on a topic, Pages let you turn those findings into a structured, shareable document — useful for reports, guides, or reference materials.

### Multiple AI Models

Perplexity is not locked into a single AI model. Depending on your plan, you can access models from several leading AI companies — Perplexity's own Sonar models, plus models from OpenAI, Anthropic, Google, and xAI. Different models have different strengths, and Perplexity lets you choose the right tool for the job.

### Comet Browser

Perplexity released its own web browser, Comet — a free, AI-powered browser that integrates Perplexity's search capabilities directly into your browsing experience. We will cover Comet in more detail later, but it represents Perplexity's vision of what web browsing looks like when AI is woven into the fabric of the experience rather than bolted on as an afterthought.

### File Uploads and Image Generation

You can upload documents, images, and other files for Perplexity to analyze. Need a summary of a PDF? Want to ask questions about a spreadsheet? You can do that. Perplexity can also generate images, making it a more versatile creative tool than a pure search engine.

## Who Is Perplexity For?

The honest answer is: almost anyone who searches the internet, which is almost everyone. But some groups benefit more immediately than others.

**Students and academics** love Perplexity because it surfaces scholarly sources efficiently and provides clear summaries that serve as starting points for deeper research. The citations make it easy to trace information back to primary sources.

**Professionals** — in business, law, finance, healthcare, or technology — use Perplexity to stay current on industry developments, research competitors, analyze data, and make informed decisions faster.

**Writers and journalists** rely on it for fact-checking, background research, and finding expert sources on unfamiliar topics.

**Curious people** — probably the largest group — use Perplexity because they want real answers to real questions without wading through SEO-optimized content farms.

If you have ever wished that searching the internet felt less like work and more like talking to a knowledgeable friend who always shows their sources, you are who Perplexity was built for.

## What This Book Will Teach You

This book is a comprehensive beginner's guide. You do not need prior experience with AI tools, and you do not need a technical background. If you can type a question, you can use Perplexity.

Over the coming chapters, you will learn how to choose the right plan, set up Perplexity on all your devices, understand and select the right AI models, craft searches that get the best results, use Focus modes and Deep Research for specialized tasks, integrate Perplexity into your daily workflow, and apply it in professional contexts.

By the end, you will not just know how to use Perplexity — you will understand how to think about AI-powered search in a way that makes you more effective at finding, evaluating, and using information. That skill will serve you well regardless of which specific tools you use in the years ahead.

## A Quick Note on AI and Trust

Before we move on, a word about trust. Perplexity is remarkably capable, but it is not infallible. No AI system is. The citations are there for a reason — they let you verify claims rather than take them on faith. Throughout this book, you will learn not just how to use Perplexity effectively but how to use it responsibly. That means checking sources, understanding limitations, and applying your own judgment to the answers you receive.

AI-powered search is a tool. A powerful one, but a tool. The goal of this book is to help you wield it skillfully.

Let's get started.

# Chapter 2: Choosing the Right Plan

## Why the Plan You Pick Actually Matters

Perplexity AI is not one of those products where the free version is crippled and the paid version is the "real" product hidden behind a paywall. The free plan is functional. You can search, get cited answers, and accomplish real work without spending a cent.

That said, the differences between plans are meaningful. The plan you choose determines which AI models you can access, how many advanced searches you can run per day, and whether you unlock features like Deep Research, Spaces, and the most powerful reasoning models available. Choosing the right plan is not about spending more for its own sake — it is about matching the tool to how you use it.

In this chapter, we will walk through every plan Perplexity offers in 2026, what each one includes, and how to decide which fits your needs.

**A note on pricing:** All prices listed in this chapter reflect Perplexity's published pricing as of early 2026. Pricing may change after publication. Check perplexity.ai for the most current plans and pricing.

## The Free Plan — A Genuine Starting Point

The Free plan gives you unlimited basic searches and five Pro Searches per day. That is not a typo — unlimited basic searches. You can ask Perplexity as many questions as you want, and every answer comes with citations. For many casual users, this is more than enough.

**What you get:**

- Unlimited basic searches with cited answers
- Five Pro Searches per day
- Access to Perplexity's default Sonar model
- Web, mobile, and desktop apps
- The Comet Browser

**What you do not get:**

- Access to premium AI models (GPT-5.4, Claude, Gemini, and others)
- Deep Research capabilities
- Higher Pro Search limits
- File upload and analysis
- Image generation
- Spaces and Pages

The five daily Pro Searches are worth highlighting. Pro Search is Perplexity's multi-step reasoning mode — it breaks complex questions into sub-queries and delivers significantly more thorough answers. Five per day handles a few important questions, but if you consistently run out by midafternoon, that is a strong signal to consider upgrading.

**Who the Free plan is for:** Casual searchers who want better answers than Google provides but do not need advanced features. Students on a tight budget who want to try before committing. Anyone evaluating whether Perplexity fits their workflow before paying.

## Pro — The Sweet Spot for Most Users

At $20/month (or $200/year, saving $40 annually), Pro is where Perplexity becomes a different tool. This is the plan most individual users will want, and it is the one I recommend as your starting point if you search the internet with any regularity.

**What you get beyond Free:**

- Significantly more Pro Searches per day
- Access to premium AI models: GPT-5.4, Claude Sonnet 4.6, Gemini 3.1 Pro, Grok 4
- Access to reasoning models: o3 and Claude Sonnet 4.0 Thinking
- Deep Research (reports, presentations, dashboards)
- File uploads and analysis
- Image generation
- Spaces and Pages

- Model Council feature

The model selection alone justifies the upgrade for many users. Instead of being limited to Perplexity's default model, you can choose from the most capable AI models available from OpenAI, Anthropic, Google, and xAI. Different models excel at different tasks, and the freedom to switch between them — which we will explore in Chapter 4 — gives you flexibility no single-model tool can match.

Deep Research is the other headline feature. When you need more than a quick answer — when you need a comprehensive investigation with a structured report — Deep Research delivers. We will cover it in depth in Chapter 12, but the short version is that it transforms Perplexity from a fast answer tool into a research platform.

**Who Pro is for:** Anyone who uses search as a meaningful part of their daily routine — students, professionals, researchers, writers, or anyone who values their time and wants the best answers available. If you spend more than 30 minutes a day searching for information online, Pro will likely save you more time than it costs.

## Max — For Power Users and Heavy Researchers

At $200/month (or $2,000/year), Max is a significant investment, designed for people who push Perplexity hard every day. This is not the plan for everyone, but for those who need it, nothing else compares.

**What you get beyond Pro:**

- The highest Pro Search limits available
- Exclusive access to top-tier models: o3-pro, Claude Opus 4, Claude Opus 4.1 Thinking
- Expanded Deep Research capabilities
- Priority access during high-demand periods
- Higher file upload limits

The exclusive models are the standout difference. Claude Opus 4 and its Thinking variant, along with o3-pro, are among the most capable AI models in existence. They excel at complex reasoning, nuanced analysis, and tasks that demand sustained, multi-step thinking. If your work regularly involves difficult analytical problems — legal research, scientific literature review, complex financial modeling, strategic analysis — the Max-exclusive models produce noticeably better results.

The pricing might cause sticker shock, but consider what it replaces. A junior research analyst costs tens of thousands of dollars per year. Professional research databases often charge hundreds or thousands monthly. If Perplexity Max saves you a few hours per week of research time, the math works out quickly for many professionals.

**Who Max is for:** Researchers, analysts, consultants, lawyers, and other professionals whose work demands the highest quality AI-assisted research. People who have used Pro extensively and consistently wish they had access to more powerful models or higher usage limits.

## Enterprise Pro — Bringing Perplexity to Your Team

At $40/seat/month, Enterprise Pro extends Pro-level capabilities to teams and organizations with additional features designed for business use.

**What you get beyond Pro:**

- Team management and administration tools
- Shared Spaces for collaborative research
- Single sign-on (SSO) integration
- Enhanced security and data handling
- Usage analytics and reporting
- Centralized billing

The collaborative features are the key differentiator. Shared Spaces let team members contribute to and build on each other's research. Administration tools let managers control access, monitor usage, and ensure the tool is being used effectively across the organization.

**Who Enterprise Pro is for:** Teams of five or more who want to standardize on Perplexity as a research and search tool. Companies that need SSO, compliance features, and centralized management. Organizations where multiple people research overlapping topics and would benefit from shared knowledge bases.

## Enterprise Max — The Full Platform

At $325/seat/month, Enterprise Max combines the most powerful models from the Max plan with the team and administrative features of Enterprise Pro. This is Perplexity's flagship offering for organizations that demand the best of everything.

**What you get beyond Enterprise Pro:**

- All Max-exclusive models (o3-pro, Claude Opus 4, Claude Opus 4.1 Thinking)
- Highest usage limits across all features
- Priority support
- Custom integrations and API access
- Advanced analytics

**Who Enterprise Max is for:** Research-intensive organizations — think consulting firms, law firms, hedge funds, R&D departments — where the quality of information analysis directly impacts revenue or outcomes. Teams where the cost of a wrong answer or missed insight far exceeds the subscription cost.

## How to Decide — A Practical Framework

If the plan descriptions above did not make your choice obvious, here is a simple framework.

**Start with Free if** you are new to Perplexity and want to explore before committing money. Use it for a week. Pay attention to how often you hit the five-Pro-Search limit. Notice whether you wish you could try different models or use Deep Research. If Free satisfies your needs after a full week, stay there.

**Upgrade to Pro if** any of the following are true: you run out of Pro Searches regularly, you want access to better AI models, you need Deep Research for school or work, or you find yourself relying on Perplexity enough that the 20-dollar monthly cost feels trivial compared to the value. For most readers of this book, Pro is where you will land.

**Upgrade to Max if** you have been on Pro for a while and find yourself wishing for more powerful models, especially for complex analytical tasks. If you are a professional whose income depends on research quality, try Max for a month and see whether the exclusive models make a material difference. For some professions, the answer will be an emphatic yes.

**Choose an Enterprise plan if** you are evaluating Perplexity for a team or organization. The collaborative features, administrative controls, and security compliance are essential for business deployment. The choice between Enterprise Pro and Enterprise Max depends on whether your team needs the most powerful models or whether Pro-level models are sufficient.

## The Subscription-Only Model — Why It Matters to You

Earlier, we mentioned that Perplexity abandoned advertising entirely in February 2026. It is worth pausing on, because it directly affects your experience as a user.

When a product is funded by advertising, its incentives are split. The company needs to keep you happy enough to keep using the product, but it also needs to serve advertisers. This creates conflicts. Search results might be influenced by paid placements. The interface might be designed to maximize engagement (and ad impressions) rather than to get you answers efficiently.

Perplexity's subscription-only model means the company makes money only when you find the product valuable enough to pay for it. No ads in your search results. No sponsored placements. No incentive to keep you searching longer than necessary — in fact, the opposite. The faster and more accurately Perplexity answers your questions, the more satisfied you are, and the more likely you are to keep paying.

This alignment between company incentives and user experience is rare on the internet, and it is one of the more compelling reasons to take Perplexity seriously as a long-term tool.

## Comet Browser and Comet Plus

One more thing worth mentioning in the context of plans: Perplexity's Comet Browser is free for everyone, regardless of whether you have a Perplexity subscription. Comet is an AI-powered web browser that integrates Perplexity's capabilities directly into your browsing experience.

Comet Plus, at $5 per month, is an optional add-on that supports publishers whose content Perplexity surfaces in its answers. If you care about the sustainability of online journalism and content creation — and you should, since Perplexity's answers are only as good as the sources they draw from — Comet Plus is a straightforward way to contribute.

We will cover Comet in more detail in a later chapter, but keep it in mind as you plan your overall Perplexity setup.

## Annual vs. Monthly Billing

Both Pro and Max offer annual billing that saves you money. Pro drops from $240/year (monthly billing) to $200/year (annual billing) — about 17 percent off. Max drops from $2,400 to $2,000 per year — the same percentage savings.

If you have used Perplexity for a month and know you want to continue, switching to annual billing is an easy win. The only reason to stick with monthly is if you are still evaluating the tool and want the flexibility to cancel without losing prepaid months.

## What I Recommend

If you are reading this book, you are interested enough in Perplexity to invest time in learning it properly. My recommendation: start with Free, use it actively for a few days, then upgrade to Pro. The jump from Free to Pro is where the biggest transformation in capability happens. The jump from Pro to Max is meaningful but more incremental.

Give Pro a full month of real use before deciding whether you need Max. And if you are evaluating Perplexity for a team, start with Enterprise Pro and let your team use it for a month before considering whether Enterprise Max is justified.

The best plan is the one that matches how you use the tool — not how you imagine you might use it, and not the most expensive option just because it exists. Use Free to explore, Pro to get serious, and Max to go all in.

In the next chapter, we will get you set up on every device you own.

# Chapter 3: Setting Up and Getting Started

## Getting Perplexity on Every Screen You Own

One of Perplexity's strengths is that it meets you wherever you are. Whether you are at your desk, on your phone, or browsing the web, there is a way to access Perplexity that fits naturally into your workflow. In this chapter, we will set up Perplexity on every platform, configure your account, and make sure you are ready to start searching effectively.

Setup is straightforward — most people are up and running in under five minutes. But a few choices and settings are worth understanding upfront, so let us go through them methodically.

## Creating Your Account

Before installing anything, you need a Perplexity account. Head to perplexity.ai in any web browser and click the sign-up button. You have several options for creating an account:

- **Google sign-in** — the fastest option if you have a Google account
- **Apple sign-in** — convenient if you are in the Apple ecosystem
- **Email and password** — the traditional approach, works for everyone

Any of these works fine. The one consideration is that your sign-in method will be how you authenticate across all your devices, so pick something you will not have trouble with on your phone, your desktop, and any other device you plan to use.

Once your account is created, you land on the Perplexity web interface. You can start searching immediately — no further setup required. But we will do more than the minimum, because the full Perplexity experience extends beyond a browser tab.

## The Web Interface

The web app at perplexity.ai is the most full-featured way to use Perplexity, and for many people, it is the primary interface. It works in any modern browser and requires no installation.

When you first load the interface, you see a clean search bar front and center. Below it, you may see trending topics or suggested searches. The left sidebar contains your search history, Spaces, and account settings.

A few things to configure right away in your account settings:

**Default model.** If you are on Pro or Max, you can set which AI model Perplexity uses by default. We will cover model selection in Chapter 4, but for now, the default Sonar model is a fine starting point. You can always override it on a per-search basis.

**Appearance.** Perplexity supports light and dark modes. Pick whichever is easier on your eyes. Trivial, but if you are going to use this tool daily, visual comfort matters.

**Language preferences.** If you primarily search in a language other than English, you can set your preferred language in the settings. Perplexity handles multilingual queries well, but setting a default can improve the consistency of results.

## Desktop Apps — Mac and Windows

Perplexity offers dedicated desktop applications for both Mac and Windows. These are not just wrappers around the web app — they provide a native experience with a few advantages.

### Why Use the Desktop App

**Speed.** The desktop app loads faster than opening a browser tab and navigating to perplexity.ai. If you search frequently throughout the day, those saved seconds add up.

**Keyboard shortcuts.** The desktop app supports system-wide keyboard shortcuts. Configure a hotkey that summons Perplexity from anywhere on your computer, type your question, and get an answer without switching away from your current work. In my opinion, this is the single best reason to install the desktop app.

**Focus.** A dedicated app means Perplexity is not competing with dozens of browser tabs for your attention. It is its own window, its own space, and that separation helps you treat it as a tool rather than another website.

### Installing on Windows

Download the Windows app from perplexity.ai or from the Microsoft Store. Run the installer, sign in with your Perplexity account, and you are done. The app will appear in your Start menu and can be pinned to your taskbar.

After installation, open the app's settings and configure the global hotkey. The default varies, but you can set it to whatever combination feels natural. Pick something you can hit without thinking — a combination that does not conflict with your other applications.

### Installing on Mac

Download the Mac app from perplexity.ai or from the Mac App Store. Install it as you would any Mac application — drag it to your Applications folder or let the App Store handle it. Sign in with your account.

On Mac, the global hotkey is particularly useful because macOS supports it natively and reliably. Configure it in the app's preferences. Many users set it to a combination using the Option key, since that key is underutilized in most workflows.

## Mobile Apps — iOS and Android

Perplexity's mobile apps are excellent, and for many users, the phone is where most of their searching happens. The mobile experience is well-designed for the constraints of a smaller screen.

### iOS

Download Perplexity from the App Store. Sign in with your account. The app integrates with iOS in several useful ways:

- **Siri Shortcuts.** Set up Siri to trigger a Perplexity search so you can ask questions by voice.
- **Share Sheet.** When you are in another app — reading an article in Safari, looking at a tweet, browsing Reddit — share content directly to Perplexity for analysis or follow-up questions.
- **Widget.** Perplexity offers a home screen widget with a search bar you can tap, skipping the step of opening the app first.

### Android

Download Perplexity from the Google Play Store. Sign in with your account. The Android app offers similar integrations:

- **Share functionality.** Share content from any app to Perplexity for analysis.
- **Widget.** A home screen widget for quick access to search.
- **Default assistant.** On some Android devices, you can set Perplexity as your default digital assistant, replacing Google Assistant for search queries.

### Mobile Tips

Regardless of which phone you use, a few tips will improve your mobile experience:

**Enable notifications** selectively. Perplexity can notify you about completed Deep Research reports and updates in your Spaces. These are useful; turn off the rest.

**Use voice input.** Both iOS and Android have excellent voice-to-text. Instead of typing on a small keyboard, tap the microphone icon and speak your question. Perplexity handles natural-language voice queries as well as typed ones.

**Save searches for later.** If you start a complex research thread on your phone but want to continue on your desktop, your search history syncs across devices automatically. No need to email yourself links or take screenshots.

## The Chrome Extension

If you spend a lot of time in Google Chrome, the Perplexity Chrome extension is worth installing. It adds Perplexity's capabilities to your browser without requiring you to navigate away from the page you are on.

Install it from the Chrome Web Store by searching for "Perplexity." Once installed, you will see a Perplexity icon in your browser toolbar.

**What the extension does:**

- **Quick search.** Click the icon or use a keyboard shortcut to open a Perplexity search panel without leaving your current tab.
- **Page context.** Highlight text on any webpage, right-click, and ask Perplexity about it. The extension sends both your question and the highlighted text as context, which often yields more relevant answers.
- **Sidebar mode.** On some pages, you can open Perplexity as a sidebar alongside the content you are reading, letting you fact-check, ask follow-up questions, or dig deeper in real time.

The extension is lightweight and does not noticeably slow down your browser. If Chrome is your primary browser and you are not ready to switch to Comet, this is the next-best thing.

## The Comet Browser

Comet is Perplexity's own web browser, and it represents the most deeply integrated Perplexity experience available. Rather than adding AI search to a browser as an extension, Comet was built from the ground up with AI search as a core feature.

**Key features of Comet:**

- **AI-native address bar.** Type a question in the address bar, and Comet routes it to Perplexity rather than a traditional search engine. Type a URL, and it navigates normally. The browser distinguishes between the two.
- **Inline answers.** When browsing any webpage, highlight text and get instant Perplexity answers without opening a new tab or sidebar.

- **Privacy focus.** Comet was designed with privacy in mind, limiting tracking and data collection beyond what the AI features require.
- **Free.** Comet is free for everyone, regardless of your Perplexity plan.

**Comet Plus**, at $5 per month, is an optional add-on that directs a portion of your subscription to the publishers whose content Perplexity cites. If you use Perplexity heavily and care about supporting the ecosystem of journalists, researchers, and writers whose work makes AI answers possible, Comet Plus is a meaningful way to give back.

Should you switch to Comet? If you are open to trying a new browser and you use Perplexity frequently, it is worth a serious look. The integration is smoother than any extension can provide. If you are deeply invested in Chrome, Firefox, or another browser's ecosystem — with years of bookmarks, extensions, and muscle memory — the Chrome extension might be the more practical choice for now.

## Configuring Your Account Settings

With Perplexity installed on your devices, take a few minutes to configure your account settings. These settings sync across all your devices, so you only need to do this once.

### Profile and Preferences

**Display name.** Set this to whatever you like. It appears in shared Spaces and collaborative features.

**Default Focus mode.** You can set a default Focus mode for your searches. We will cover Focus modes in Chapter 7, but the default "Web" mode is the right starting point for most people.

**Output language.** If you want responses in a specific language, set it here. Perplexity can respond in dozens of languages regardless of the language you ask in.

### Privacy Settings

**Search history.** By default, Perplexity saves your search history so you can return to previous conversations. You can disable this if privacy is a concern, but doing so means you also lose the ability to continue previous search threads.

**Data usage.** Review the data usage settings to understand what information Perplexity retains and how it is used. The company is generally transparent here, and the privacy policy is written in more accessible language than most.

### Notification Settings

Configure notifications on each device. I recommend enabling notifications for completed Deep Research reports (since they can take a few minutes to generate) and disabling most other notifications to avoid distraction.

## Your First Search — A Quick Preview

With everything set up, let us do a quick test. Open Perplexity on whichever device you prefer and type a simple question into the search bar. Something factual and current works well — try "What were the major tech news stories this week?" or "What is the current weather in [your city]?"

You should see a response within a few seconds. It will be written in clear prose, with numbered citations throughout the text. Each number corresponds to a source listed at the bottom of the response. Click one — it should take you to the original webpage where that information was found.

If all of that works, you are fully set up. In Chapter 4, we will take a closer look at the AI models powering your searches, and in Chapter 5, we will dig into how to craft searches that get you the best possible answers.

## Troubleshooting Common Setup Issues

Most people set up Perplexity without any problems, but a few issues come up occasionally:

**"I cannot sign in on my second device."** Make sure you are using the same sign-in method (Google, Apple, or email) on all devices. If you signed up with Google on your laptop and try to sign in with email on your phone, the system treats you as a different user.

**"The desktop app will not install."** Check your operating system version. Perplexity's desktop apps require relatively recent versions of Windows and macOS. If you are running an older OS, the web interface at perplexity.ai is a fully functional alternative.

**“My Pro features are not showing up.”** If you recently upgraded your plan, try signing out and back in. Plan changes sometimes take a moment to propagate across devices.

**“The Chrome extension conflicts with another extension.”** Some ad blockers and privacy extensions interfere with the Perplexity extension. If you experience issues, try disabling other extensions one at a time to identify the conflict.

If you run into something not covered here, Perplexity’s help center is searchable and regularly updated. You can also ask Perplexity itself for help — it handles questions about its own features surprisingly well.

You are set up. The next chapter shows how to choose the right model for the questions you ask.

# Part II: Understanding Perplexity

---

*"Google can bring you back 100,000 answers. A librarian can bring you back the right one."*

— Neil Gaiman

---

# Chapter 4: Understanding Perplexity's Models

## Why the Model You Choose Matters

When you ask Perplexity a question, an AI model does the heavy lifting — reading the search results, reasoning through the information, and composing your answer. Here is something many new users do not realize: Perplexity does not use just one model. Depending on your plan, you have access to a lineup of models from several different companies, each with distinct strengths.

Choosing the right model for a given task can be the difference between a good answer and a great one. You do not need a computer science degree to make smart choices here — you just need to know what each model does well and when to reach for it. That is what this chapter is about.

## What Is a Language Model, Briefly

A language model is software trained on enormous amounts of text — books, articles, websites, code, conversations — until it develops the ability to understand and generate human language. When you ask a question, the model does not "look up" an answer in a database. It processes your question, considers the context (including any web search results Perplexity feeds it), and generates a response word by word.

Different models are built by different companies using different training approaches, different data, and different optimization goals. That is why they behave differently. A model built to be cautious and precise responds differently from one built to be creative and expansive, even given the same question and the same source material.

In Perplexity, the model works in tandem with the search engine. Perplexity's search infrastructure finds the relevant sources; the model reads those sources and composes the answer. Think of Perplexity as the research department and the model as the analyst writing the report.

## Perplexity's Own Models — The Sonar Family

Perplexity develops its own models under the Sonar brand. These are based on Meta's Llama architecture and have been optimized for search and retrieval — meaning they are particularly good at reading web content and synthesizing it into clear answers.

**Sonar** is the default model on the Free plan and the baseline option on paid plans. It is fast, capable, and well-suited for the vast majority of everyday searches. When you need a quick, accurate answer to a straightforward question, Sonar handles it efficiently.

The advantage of Sonar is that it was built for Perplexity's use case. The other available models are general-purpose systems adapted to work with Perplexity's search infrastructure; Sonar was designed from the start as a search synthesis engine. That makes it efficient — it produces concise, well-cited answers quickly.

**When to use Sonar:** Factual questions, quick lookups, news summaries, straightforward research. Anytime speed and efficiency matter more than depth of reasoning.

## OpenAI Models — GPT-5.4 and o3

OpenAI is the company behind ChatGPT, and their models are some of the most widely used in the world. Perplexity gives Pro and Max subscribers access to several of them.

### GPT-5.4

GPT-5.4 is OpenAI's flagship general-purpose model, the current iteration in the GPT-5 family. It is a strong all-rounder — good at understanding complex questions, generating well-structured responses, and handling a wide range of topics from creative writing to technical analysis.

GPT-5.4 incorporates refinements over earlier GPT-5 releases. The differences are more evolutionary than revolutionary, but it is the version Perplexity surfaces by default in the GPT lineup.

**When to use GPT-5.4:** Complex questions that require nuanced understanding, writing or communication tasks, situations where you want a well-rounded response that balances depth with readability.

### o3 and o3-pro

The "o" in o3 stands for reasoning. OpenAI's o-series models are designed to think through problems step by step before responding. Instead of generating an answer immediately, o3 takes additional time to reason through the problem, consider multiple approaches, and arrive at a more careful conclusion.

The standard o3 model is available to Pro and Max subscribers. o3-pro, the more powerful variant, is exclusive to Max subscribers.

**When to use o3:** Math problems, logic puzzles, complex analytical questions, anything where step-by-step reasoning improves the answer. If another model's answer seems superficial or misses important nuances, try o3.

**When to use o3-pro (Max only):** The hardest analytical and reasoning tasks you encounter. Scientific analysis, complex financial modeling, multi-variable decisions. o3-pro takes longer to respond but produces more thorough reasoning chains.

## Anthropic Models — Claude Sonnet and Opus

Anthropic builds the Claude family of models. They are known for being thoughtful, thorough, and particularly good at following nuanced instructions.

### Claude Sonnet 4.6

Claude Sonnet 4.6 is available on Pro and Max plans. It is a strong general-purpose model that many users find produces particularly well-written and well-organized responses. Sonnet is thorough without being verbose — it covers what needs to be covered and structures information clearly.

**When to use Claude Sonnet 4.6:** Research questions where you want well-organized, comprehensive answers. Writing tasks. Situations where clarity of expression matters. Many users find Claude Sonnet their preferred default for day-to-day use.

### Claude Sonnet 4.0 Thinking

This is a reasoning-enhanced version of Claude Sonnet. Like OpenAI's o3, it spends additional time thinking through problems before responding. Available on Pro and Max plans.

**When to use Claude Sonnet 4.0 Thinking:** Complex reasoning tasks where you want Claude's writing quality combined with step-by-step problem-solving. Analytical questions that benefit from deliberate reasoning.

### Claude Opus 4 and Claude Opus 4.1 Thinking (Max Only)

Claude Opus is Anthropic's most powerful model line. Opus 4 and Opus 4.1 Thinking are exclusive to Max subscribers and represent the peak of what Claude can do.

Opus models excel at tasks requiring deep understanding, nuanced judgment, and sustained reasoning over long contexts. They shine when the question is ambiguous, the answer requires weighing competing considerations, or the topic demands expert-level analysis.

**When to use Claude Opus (Max only):** The most challenging research and analysis tasks. Legal analysis, medical literature review, philosophical arguments, strategic planning — any situation where you want the most thoughtful, thorough answer possible and are willing to wait a bit longer for it.

## Google Models — Gemini 3.1 Pro

Google's Gemini models are notable for strong performance across multiple modalities — text, images, code, and more. Gemini 3.1 Pro is available on Pro and Max plans.

Gemini 3.1 Pro is particularly strong at data analysis, mathematical reasoning, and tasks where the answer benefits from Google's deep knowledge base. It also handles multilingual queries exceptionally well.

**When to use Gemini 3.1 Pro:** Data-heavy research, mathematical questions, multilingual searches, code analysis. Gemini is also a strong choice when you want a second opinion on an answer from another model — its training and optimization are different enough that it often surfaces different perspectives.

## xAI Models — Grok 4

Grok 4 is built by xAI, the AI company founded by Elon Musk. Available on Pro and Max plans. Grok has a reputation for being direct and willing to engage with topics other models handle more cautiously.

**When to use Grok 4:** When you want a direct, no-hedging answer. When you are researching topics where you feel other models are being overly cautious or piling on caveats. Grok can also be strong for current events analysis, particularly around technology, business, and politics.

## The Model Council

One of Perplexity's more innovative features is the Model Council, available to Pro and Max subscribers. Instead of choosing a single model for your query, the Model Council sends your question to multiple models simultaneously and synthesizes their responses into a unified answer.

This is particularly powerful when different models might have different strengths. A factual question about a complex topic might get better source analysis from one model and a better explanation from another. The Model Council combines these strengths.

**When to use Model Council:** High-stakes research where accuracy is critical. Questions where you want multiple perspectives synthesized rather than relying on a single model's interpretation. Situations where you do not know which model would perform best and want to hedge your bets.

The trade-off is speed — the Model Council takes longer than a single model because it runs multiple queries in parallel. For quick lookups, it is overkill. For important research, it is a real advantage.

## How to Choose — A Practical Guide

If the number of options feels overwhelming, here is a simple decision framework:

**For everyday questions** — factual lookups, news, general curiosity — use Sonar or your preferred default model. Speed matters here, and any model will handle these well.

**For important research** — school assignments, work projects, decisions with consequences — use Claude Sonnet 4.6 or GPT-5.4. Both produce thorough, well-structured answers.

**For hard reasoning problems** — math, logic, complex analysis — use o3, Claude Sonnet 4.0 Thinking, or (if you have Max) o3-pro or Claude Opus 4.1 Thinking.

**For critical decisions** — when you need the highest confidence in the answer — use the Model Council.

**For experimentation** — try different models on the same question. You will quickly develop intuitions about which models you prefer for which tasks. Everyone's preferences are slightly different, and the best way to discover yours is through experience.

## Changing Your Model

Switching models is easy. In the search interface, you will see a model selector near the search bar — a dropdown or an icon you click. Pick the model you want before submitting your search. You can also change your default model in account settings so your preferred model is always pre-selected.

Within a conversation thread, you can switch models between follow-up questions. This is useful if you started with a fast model for initial research and want to switch to a reasoning model for deeper analysis of what you found.

## A Note on Model Speed and Quality

There is a trade-off between speed and depth of reasoning. Sonar and the standard versions of GPT and Claude respond in a few seconds. Reasoning models like o3 and the Thinking variants take longer — sometimes significantly longer for complex questions. The most powerful Max-exclusive models may take the longest of all.

This trade-off is expected. A model that spends more time thinking typically produces better answers for complex questions. But for simple factual queries, the extra thinking adds latency without meaningfully improving the answer. Match the model to the task, and you will get the best balance of speed and quality.

Now that you understand what is under the hood, let us put it to work. In the next chapter, you will run your first real searches and learn how to get the most out of every query.

# Chapter 5: Your First Searches

## Learning to Ask the Right Way

You already know how to use a search engine. You have been typing queries into Google for years, maybe decades. But Perplexity is not Google, and the habits you built around traditional search can hold you back here. The good news is that searching effectively on Perplexity is not harder — it is different, and in most ways, more natural.

In this chapter, you will learn how to craft queries that get the best results from Perplexity, how to use follow-up questions to dig deeper, when to reach for Pro Search, and how to read and evaluate the answers you get back.

## Forget Keyword-Speak

The most important mindset shift: stop writing search queries and start asking questions.

On Google, you were trained to strip your thoughts down to keywords. Instead of "What are the health benefits of drinking green tea daily?" you learned to type "green tea health benefits daily." That keyword compression is a skill you developed because traditional search engines match words, not meaning.

Perplexity understands meaning. It is backed by language models that comprehend full sentences, context, nuance, and intent. Ask a complete question in natural language and you give it more to work with — and get better results.

Compare these two approaches:

**Keyword style:** "best laptop 2026 under 1000"

**Natural language:** "What is the best laptop I can buy in 2026 for under 1000 dollars if I mainly use it for writing, web browsing, and occasional video editing?"

The second query gives Perplexity enough context to tailor its answer to your specific needs. The first forces it to guess what you care about — and it will probably give you a generic "top 10" response.

This does not mean keywords never work. For simple factual lookups — "population of Japan 2026" or "boiling point of ethanol" — a concise query is fine. But when your question has nuance, context, or specific needs, use full sentences. Talk to Perplexity the way you would talk to a knowledgeable colleague.

## Your First Basic Search

Let's start with a simple search to see how Perplexity works in practice.

Open Perplexity on whatever device you prefer. In the search bar, type:

**"What are the main differences between type 1 and type 2 diabetes?"**

Hit enter (or tap the search button on mobile). Within a few seconds, you will see a response. Let's examine what you get back.

**The answer itself** will be a clear prose explanation covering the key differences — causes, age of onset, treatment approaches, and other relevant factors. It reads like a paragraph from a health encyclopedia, not a list of search results.

**Citations** appear as small numbered references throughout the text. You might see something like "Type 1 diabetes is an autoimmune condition [1] in which the body's immune system attacks insulin-producing cells [2]." Those numbers link to specific sources — medical websites, research institutions, health organizations.

**Source list** at the bottom shows the full URLs and titles of every cited source. Click any to read the original material.

**Follow-up suggestions** may appear below the answer. Perplexity often suggests related questions you might want to explore next. These are useful and often anticipate exactly what you would want to know after reading the initial answer.

**Related images or media** might appear if they are relevant to your query. For a medical question, you might see a diagram or infographic.

Click one or two of the citations. This is not just a verification step — it is how you build trust in the tool. Over time, you will develop a sense for how accurately Perplexity represents its sources.

## The Power of Follow-Up Questions

One of Perplexity's greatest strengths is conversational continuity. After you get an answer, you can ask follow-up questions, and Perplexity remembers the context.

Continuing our diabetes example, you might follow up with:

- "Which type is more common?"
- "What are the early warning signs of type 2?"
- "How has treatment for type 1 changed in the last five years?"

Each follow-up draws on both new search results and the context of your conversation. Perplexity understands that "which type" refers to the diabetes types you were just discussing. No need to repeat background information.

This conversational flow is where Perplexity outperforms traditional search most dramatically. On Google, each new query starts from scratch. On Perplexity, each follow-up builds on what came before, creating a deepening thread of understanding.

**Tips for effective follow-ups:**

- Be specific about what you want to know next
- Reference the previous answer when it helps — "You mentioned that type 2 is linked to lifestyle factors. Which lifestyle changes have the strongest evidence?"
- Do not hesitate to challenge the answer — "Are there studies that contradict what you just said?"
- Ask for clarification if something was unclear — "Can you explain the autoimmune mechanism in simpler terms?"

## When to Use Pro Search

Basic search handles most questions well, but some benefit from Pro Search's multi-step reasoning. Knowing when to use it will make you a more effective researcher.

**Basic search** does a single search, reads the results, and writes an answer. It is fast — usually a few seconds — and works well for questions with straightforward, readily available answers.

**Pro Search** breaks complex questions into sub-queries, searches multiple times, evaluates the results, and sometimes refines its approach based on what it finds. It takes longer — typically 15 to 30 seconds — but produces more thorough, nuanced answers.

Use Pro Search when:

- The question is complex or multi-part
- You need a comprehensive overview, not just a quick answer
- The topic is nuanced and different sources might say different things
- You are doing research that will inform a decision
- A basic search gave you an answer that felt incomplete

Use basic search when:

- You need a quick factual answer
- The question is straightforward
- Speed matters more than depth
- You are doing initial exploration and do not yet know what you need in detail

**Example where Pro Search shines:** "What are the pros and cons of moving from a traditional IRA to a Roth IRA in 2026, considering the current tax brackets and the proposed legislative changes?"

This question involves multiple domains — tax law, financial planning, current legislation — and the best answer requires synthesizing information from several different sources. Pro Search will break this into sub-queries, search for current tax brackets, proposed legislation, and IRA conversion strategies separately, and combine everything into a coherent analysis.

**Example where basic search is fine:** "What is the current federal funds rate?"

One search, one answer, done.

## Crafting Better Queries — Practical Techniques

Beyond the general principle of using natural language, here are specific techniques that consistently improve Perplexity's responses.

### Provide Context About Why You Are Asking

"What is a good protein intake?" is vague. "What is a good daily protein intake for a 40-year-old man who weight trains three times a week and wants to build muscle?" gives Perplexity everything it needs to deliver a targeted answer.

### Specify the Format You Want

If you want a comparison, ask for one: "Compare the Samsung Galaxy S26 and iPhone 17 in terms of camera quality, battery life, and price."

If you want a list, say so: "List the five most common causes of lower back pain and briefly explain each one."

If you want a step-by-step explanation: "Walk me through the process of setting up a sole proprietorship in California, step by step."

### Set the Level of Expertise

"Explain quantum entanglement" gives you a general-audience explanation. "Explain quantum entanglement as you would to a physics undergraduate" gives you something more technical. "Explain quantum entanglement to a five-year-old" gives you something simpler. Perplexity adjusts based on the audience you specify.

### Constrain the Scope When Needed

If you want recent information: "What have been the major developments in CRISPR gene therapy in the past six months?"

If you want a specific geographic focus: "What are the current immigration requirements for US citizens moving to Portugal?"

If you want a specific type of source: "According to peer-reviewed research, what is the evidence for meditation reducing anxiety?"

### Ask for Balanced Perspectives

"What are both the arguments for and against a four-day work week, based on recent studies and real-world implementations?"

An explicit request for balance helps Perplexity avoid presenting only one side of a debatable topic.

## Reading Perplexity's Answers Critically

Perplexity is a tool, not an oracle. Reading its answers with critical thinking is an essential skill.

### Check the Citations

Not all sources are equal. A citation from the Mayo Clinic, a peer-reviewed journal, or an official government database carries more weight than a citation from a random blog post or content farm. Perplexity tells you where its information comes from — use that transparency.

### Watch for Hedging Language

When Perplexity says "research suggests" or "some experts argue," it is signaling that the evidence is not conclusive or that sources disagree. Pay attention to this hedging — it is Perplexity being honest about uncertainty, and that honesty is valuable.

### Notice What Is Missing

Sometimes the most important thing about an answer is what it does not say. If you ask about a controversial topic and the response seems to present only one perspective, ask a follow-up specifically requesting the other side. No single search query will always capture every relevant viewpoint.

### Verify High-Stakes Information

If you are making a medical, legal, or financial decision — or any decision with significant consequences — do not rely solely on Perplexity's answer. Use it as a starting point, then verify critical details with authoritative sources: a doctor, a lawyer, an accountant, official institutional websites.

This is not a weakness specific to Perplexity — it is common sense about any information source, including traditional search engines. The difference is that Perplexity makes verification easier by providing citations upfront.

## Common Beginner Mistakes

Having helped many people get started with Perplexity, here are the mistakes I see most often:

**Using it like Google.** Keyword-only queries, treating each search as independent rather than building conversational threads, not asking follow-ups. Perplexity rewards natural language and iterative inquiry.

**Never using Pro Search.** Some users stick with basic search for everything, even complex research questions. If you are on a paid plan, Pro Search is one of the most valuable features — use it when the question warrants it.

**Accepting the first answer without follow-up.** The first answer is often a starting point. The best answers come from a conversation — asking follow-ups, requesting clarification, pushing for more depth on specific points.

**Not checking citations.** The citations are there for a reason. Clicking through to sources occasionally improves your trust calibration and sometimes leads you to valuable original material beyond what Perplexity summarized.

**Asking overly broad questions.** "Tell me about AI" is too broad for any tool to answer well. "What are the three most significant developments in AI regulation in the European Union in 2025 and 2026?" is specific enough to get a useful answer.

## Practice Exercises

The best way to learn is by doing. Here are five searches to try that exercise different aspects of what we have covered:

1. **Factual lookup with follow-ups.** Search for "How does mRNA vaccine technology work?" Then ask three follow-up questions to deepen your understanding.

2. **Comparison query.** Ask Perplexity to compare two products, cities, investment strategies, or anything else you are curious about. Pay attention to how it structures the comparison.
3. **Pro Search deep dive.** Use Pro Search to investigate a complex topic — something like "What are the leading theories about why productivity growth has slowed in developed economies since the 1970s?"
4. **Current events.** Ask about something that happened in the news today. Notice how the citations are all recent and how the answer reflects current information rather than outdated training data.
5. **Opinion-dependent question.** Ask about something where reasonable people disagree — a policy question, a lifestyle choice, a business strategy. See how Perplexity handles presenting multiple perspectives.

As you work through these, watch the patterns. Notice which types of queries get the best responses, how follow-ups refine the answers, and how your searching instincts develop. By the end of these five exercises, you will already be searching more effectively than most Perplexity users.

In the next chapter, we will take your searching to the next level with Perplexity's research tools — including a preview of features like Deep Research, Spaces, and Pages that we will explore in depth later in the book.

# Part III: Core Use Cases

---

*"If we knew what it was we were doing, it would not be called research, would it?"*

— Albert Einstein (attributed)

---

# Chapter 6: Research with Perplexity

## Beyond Quick Answers — Real Research

In the previous chapter, you learned how to get clear, cited answers to your questions. That alone makes Perplexity a powerful daily tool. But Perplexity's ambitions go further. Its research features — particularly Deep Research, Spaces, and Pages — transform it from an answer engine into a research platform capable of producing work that would have taken a human researcher hours or days.

This chapter is about moving from asking questions to conducting research. The skills you build here will serve you whether you are writing a school paper, evaluating a business opportunity, planning a major purchase, or satisfying curiosity about a complex topic.

## A Preview of What Is Ahead

Before we build a research workflow, it is worth knowing that Perplexity offers several powerful features we will cover in dedicated chapters later in the book. Here is a brief orientation so you know what is available and where to find the full treatment.

**Deep Research** is Perplexity's most thorough investigation mode. Instead of a single search, it runs a multi-stage process — breaking your question into sub-queries, searching dozens of sources, evaluating and cross-referencing what it finds, and producing comprehensive reports, presentations, or dashboards. If you have ever wished you could hand a complex research question to a tireless assistant and get back a structured briefing, Deep Research is that tool. We cover it fully in Chapter 12.

**Spaces** give you persistent, organized workspaces for ongoing projects. You can collect related searches, upload reference files, set custom instructions that shape every response, and invite collaborators. Think of a Space as a dedicated research room where the AI already knows your project's context. Chapter 10 covers creating, configuring, and getting the most out of Spaces.

**Pages** transform your research into polished, shareable web content — structured documents with sections, citations, and a clean layout that anyone can access, even without a Perplexity account. When you need to turn findings into a deliverable, Pages give you a head start. Chapter 11 has the full walkthrough.

**File uploads** let you bring your own documents — PDFs, spreadsheets, Word files, images — into Perplexity for analysis. You can ask questions about uploaded files, combine them with web search, and extract insights from private data that would never surface in a web search. Chapter 13 covers everything you can do with file uploads.

## Building a Research Workflow

Now that you understand the individual tools, here is how to combine them into an effective research workflow:

### Step 1: Initial Exploration

Start with a few basic or Pro Searches to orient yourself. What are the key terms? Who are the major voices? What are the main subtopics? This is not about finding answers yet — it is about understanding the landscape.

### Step 2: Create a Space

Once you have a sense of the topic, create a Space for your project. From this point forward, conduct all related searches within this Space.

### Step 3: Deep Research

Launch a Deep Research query with a well-scoped question. Let it generate a comprehensive report. Read the report carefully, noting areas where you want more depth.

### Step 4: Targeted Follow-Ups

Use Pro Search and basic search to dig into specific aspects the Deep Research report surfaced. Ask follow-up questions. Challenge findings. Seek alternative perspectives.

### Step 5: Integrate External Materials

If you have relevant documents — papers, data, interview notes — upload them to Perplexity and ask it to integrate their content with what it has already found.

### Step 6: Synthesize with Pages

When you are ready to produce a deliverable, use Pages to organize your findings into a coherent document. Edit and refine the output to match your needs.

### Step 7: Verify and Finalize

Before treating any research as complete, verify the critical claims by checking cited sources directly. For high-stakes work, cross-reference key findings with authoritative sources outside of what Perplexity surfaced.

## Research Ethics and Best Practices

A few important notes about using Perplexity for research:

**Cite your sources properly.** If you are using Perplexity's research in academic work, professional reports, or published content, cite the original sources — not Perplexity itself. Perplexity makes this easy by providing citations, but the responsibility for attribution is yours.

**Do not treat AI-generated research as a substitute for primary research.** Perplexity excels at synthesizing existing information. It cannot conduct original experiments, interviews, or observations. For research that requires primary data, use Perplexity to inform your approach and contextualize your findings, not to replace the work itself.

**Be aware of source bias.** Perplexity searches the web, and the web has biases. English-language sources dominate. Popular viewpoints are overrepresented. Recent publications carry more weight than older ones. Stay conscious of these biases, especially when researching topics where marginalized perspectives or non-English-language scholarship matter.

**Keep records.** Spaces help with this, but develop the habit of saving important research conversations. Perplexity's results can change over time as web content evolves, so if a finding matters, record it along with the source.

Perplexity gives you a research assistant that never sleeps, never tires, and works at extraordinary speed. Your job is to direct it well and think critically about what it finds. In the next chapter, we will explore Focus modes — specialized lenses that point Perplexity's search at exactly the type of information you need.

# Chapter 7: Focus Modes

## Pointing the Spotlight Where It Matters

By default, Perplexity casts a wide net across the entire web. That is usually the right approach — you want the best answer from wherever it might come. But sometimes you know exactly what kind of information you need, and a broad search wastes time on irrelevant results.

Focus modes solve this problem. They narrow Perplexity's search to specific types of content and sources, so the answers draw from the most relevant corners of the internet. Think of them as specialized lenses you swap in and out depending on what you are after.

Perplexity offers six Focus modes in 2026: Web, Academic, Writing, Video, Social, and Finance. Each one changes where Perplexity searches and how it processes the results. In this chapter, we walk through every mode, explain when each one shines, and show you how to fold them into your workflow.

## How to Switch Focus Modes

Before we get into the individual modes, a quick note on access. In the search interface — web, desktop, or mobile — you will see a Focus selector near the search bar. It might appear as a dropdown, a row of icons, or a button labeled with the current mode. Click or tap it to see all available modes, then select the one you want before submitting your search.

You can change Focus mode between searches within the same conversation thread. You can also set a default Focus mode in your account settings, though I recommend leaving it on Web and switching manually when you need something specific.

## Web — The Default All-Rounder

**What it searches:** The entire open web — news sites, blogs, corporate websites, government databases, forums, Wikipedia, and everything else indexed by major search engines.

**When to use it:** When you do not know what type of source will have the best answer, or when your question could be answered by many types of content. This is the right mode for most everyday searches.

Web Focus is the default for good reason. Most questions are best answered by drawing from the widest possible range of sources. A question about a historical event might benefit from a Wikipedia article, a university page, a news archive, and a book excerpt. Web Focus finds all of them.

**Example queries for Web Focus:**

- "What caused the 2008 financial crisis?"
- "How do I fix a leaking kitchen faucet?"
- "What are the current visa requirements for Americans traveling to Brazil?"
- "Compare the nutritional profiles of quinoa and brown rice"

If you are unsure which Focus mode to use, Web is always a safe choice.

## Academic — Scholarly Sources First

**What it searches:** Academic databases, peer-reviewed journals, university repositories, research papers, scholarly articles, and scientific publications. Sources like PubMed, Semantic Scholar, arXiv, and institutional repositories are prioritized.

**When to use it:** When you need evidence-based answers grounded in research, when you are writing a paper that requires academic citations, when you want the scientific consensus on a topic, or when you are looking for specific studies and data.

Academic Focus is transformative for students, researchers, and anyone who values evidence over opinion. Instead of sifting through blog posts and news articles to find the underlying research, Academic Focus takes you straight to the source.

**Example queries for Academic Focus:**

- "What does the research say about the effectiveness of cognitive behavioral therapy for insomnia?"

- "What are the latest peer-reviewed studies on microplastics in drinking water?"
- "Find recent papers on the relationship between gut microbiome and mental health"
- "What is the current scientific understanding of dark matter?"

### Tips for Academic Focus

**Use technical terminology when you know it.** Academic Focus searches scholarly databases, so the precise terms researchers use surface more relevant results. "Neuroplasticity following traumatic brain injury" outperforms "brain recovery after head injury."

**Ask about specific methodologies.** "What randomized controlled trials have been conducted on intermittent fasting and cardiovascular health?" finds more targeted results than "is intermittent fasting good for your heart?"

**Request meta-analyses and systematic reviews.** These are the gold standard of academic evidence — studies that synthesize the findings of many other studies. "Are there systematic reviews on the effectiveness of mindfulness-based stress reduction?" points you toward the most authoritative evidence.

**Be aware of limitations.** Academic Focus searches what is available in academic databases. Recent research may not be indexed yet. Some papers sit behind paywalls, meaning Perplexity can cite them and summarize their abstracts but cannot access the full text. And scholarly sources, while rigorous, can be narrow in scope — they answer specific research questions, not necessarily the broader practical question you might be asking.

## Writing — Your Creative and Editing Partner

**What it searches:** Writing Focus differs from the other Focus modes in an important way — it does not primarily search the web. Instead, it optimizes the language model for text generation and editing tasks. Think of it less as a search tool and more as a writing assistant that happens to live inside Perplexity.

**When to use it:** When you need help drafting, editing, rewriting, or polishing text. When you want to brainstorm ideas, break through writer's block, adjust tone, or restructure a piece of writing.

Writing Focus is where Perplexity shifts from researcher to collaborator. Give it a rough draft and ask it to polish the language. Describe what you want to write and ask for a first draft. Paste in a paragraph and ask it to make it more concise, more formal, more casual, or more persuasive.

**Example queries for Writing Focus:**

- "Help me write a professional email declining a meeting invitation without being rude"
- "Rewrite this paragraph to be more concise: [paste paragraph]"
- "I need to write a cover letter for a data analyst position at a healthcare company. Here is my background: [details]"
- "Brainstorm five different opening paragraphs for an essay about the ethics of artificial intelligence"

### Tips for Writing Focus

**Provide context about audience and purpose.** "Write an explanation of blockchain" produces something generic. "Write an explanation of blockchain for a real estate industry newsletter, keeping it under 200 words and avoiding technical jargon" produces something you can use.

**Iterate.** The first draft is rarely the final draft. Ask for revisions: "Make it shorter," "Add more specific examples," "Change the tone to be more conversational." Writing Focus excels at iterative refinement.

**Use it for editing, not just creation.** Paste in your own writing and ask for feedback: "What is weak about this paragraph?" or "How can I make this argument more persuasive?" The model's perspective can catch issues you have become blind to.

## Video — Searching the Visual Web

**What it searches:** Video platforms, primarily YouTube but also other video hosting services. It searches video titles, descriptions, transcripts, and metadata.

**When to use it:** When you learn better from video than text, when you want tutorials and demonstrations, when you are looking for lectures, interviews, or visual explanations.

Video Focus is particularly useful for topics that are inherently visual — how to tie a specific knot, what a cooking technique looks like, how to perform a software task with a complex interface. It is also valuable for finding lectures, conference talks, and interviews on specialized topics.

**Example queries for Video Focus:**

- "Find the best video tutorials on learning to play fingerstyle guitar"
- "Video explaining how CRISPR gene editing works"
- "Recent conference talks about large language model safety"
- "Video demonstrations of proper deadlift form"

Perplexity summarizes the relevant videos it finds, often including timestamps for specific sections. That saves you from watching an entire 45-minute video to find the three minutes that matter.

## Social — The Voice of the People

**What it searches:** Social media platforms and community forums, including Reddit, X (formerly Twitter), discussion boards, and other user-generated content platforms.

**When to use it:** When you want real-world opinions and experiences, when you want to know what people think about a product, service, or idea, when official sources might be biased and you want unfiltered perspectives.

Social Focus is the antidote to polished marketing copy and corporate-speak. If you want to know whether a product is any good, what living in a particular city is like, or how people feel about a new policy, Social Focus cuts through the curated surface of the internet to find human perspectives.

**Example queries for Social Focus:**

- "What do people think about the Tesla Model Y after owning one for a year?"
- "Reddit discussions about the best neighborhoods to live in Portland, Oregon"
- "What are people saying about the new iPhone battery life?"

- "Real experiences with intermittent fasting from people who tried it for six months"

### Tips for Social Focus

**Remember that social media is not representative.** Reddit skews younger, more male, and more tech-savvy than the general population. X has its own demographic skews. The opinions you find in Social Focus are real, but they are not a random sample of all people.

**Look for patterns, not individual opinions.** Any single Reddit comment might be an outlier. When ten different people in ten different threads say the same thing, that is a signal worth taking seriously.

**Use Social Focus for qualitative research.** It excels at how people talk about, experience, and feel about things. It is less useful for factual claims, which should be verified through Web or Academic Focus.

## Finance — Markets, Filings, and Corporate Data

**What it searches:** Financial databases, SEC filings, corporate earnings reports, market data, financial news, analyst reports, and economic data sources.

**When to use it:** When you need financial information about companies, markets, or the economy. When you want data from official corporate filings rather than news articles about those filings.

Finance Focus is a specialist's tool. It goes beyond general financial news to access the primary source material financial professionals rely on — actual SEC filings, earnings transcripts, balance sheet data, and institutional economic reports.

**Example queries for Finance Focus:**

- "What were Apple's revenue and profit margins in the most recent quarter?"
- "Compare the debt-to-equity ratios of Ford and GM"
- "What did the Federal Reserve say in its most recent policy statement?"
- "What are the key risk factors disclosed in Nvidia's latest 10-K filing?"

### Tips for Finance Focus

**Be specific about time periods.** Financial data is meaningless without context. "What is Tesla's revenue?" is less useful than "What was Tesla's quarterly revenue for each quarter of 2025?"

**Ask about trends, not just snapshots.** "How has Amazon's operating margin changed over the past five years?" tells you more than a single data point.

**Cross-reference with Social Focus.** Finance Focus gives you the official numbers; Social Focus gives you what investors and analysts are saying about those numbers. Both perspectives matter.

## Combining Focus Modes in a Research Workflow

The real power of Focus modes emerges when you combine them inside a single research project. Here is an example of how you might use multiple modes to research a topic thoroughly.

**Topic: Should you invest in a specific company's stock?**

1. **Finance Focus:** "What are [Company]'s financials for the past three years? Revenue growth, profit margins, debt levels."
2. **Academic Focus:** "What does recent research say about the growth potential of [Company's industry]?"
3. **Social Focus:** "What are investors and analysts on Reddit and X saying about [Company]'s prospects?"
4. **Web Focus:** "What are the major risks and opportunities facing [Company] in 2026?"
5. **Video Focus:** "Recent analyst interviews or conference presentations about [Company]"

Each mode contributes a different perspective, and together they give you a far more complete picture than any single mode could.

## Setting Your Default and Switching Quickly

Most people should leave their default Focus mode set to Web. It is the most versatile and the right choice for most searches. Switch to specialized modes deliberately when you know you need a specific type of information.

Over time, switching becomes automatic. You think "I want the research on this" and reach for Academic. You think "I wonder what people actually experience" and reach for Social. The Focus modes become part of your information-seeking intuition, not an extra step.

In the next chapter, we look at how to weave Perplexity into your everyday life — replacing and improving the dozens of small searches you do without thinking.

# Chapter 8: Everyday Search and Productivity

## Making Perplexity Part of Your Daily Life

The previous chapters focused on Perplexity's big features — Deep Research, Focus modes, model selection. These capabilities matter. But most of the value you will get from Perplexity comes not from occasional Deep Research sessions but from the dozens of small searches you do every day.

What should I make for dinner with the ingredients I have? Is this a good deal on a used car? How do I remove a red wine stain from a white shirt? What time does the pharmacy close? Why does my cat keep knocking things off the counter?

These are the questions that make up the texture of daily life, and they are exactly where Perplexity replaces the tedious ritual of clicking through search results with something fast, direct, and useful. In this chapter, we look at how to use Perplexity as your default tool for everyday questions and how it can boost your personal productivity.

## Replacing Google — The Daily Habit Shift

If you have been using Google for twenty years, the switch to Perplexity requires a small but meaningful habit change. The easiest way to make it stick is to remove friction.

**Set Perplexity as your default.** If you are using the Comet Browser, this happens automatically. In Chrome, the Perplexity extension can intercept searches from the address bar. On your phone, put the Perplexity widget on your home screen. On your desktop, configure the global hotkey so Perplexity is always one keystroke away.

**Commit to a trial period.** Promise yourself one week where you try Perplexity first for every search. Not exclusively — if Perplexity does not handle something well, go to Google. But start with Perplexity. After a week, you will have a clear sense of which searches it handles better and which ones still benefit from a traditional search engine.

**The types of searches where Perplexity excels over Google:**

- Questions with definitive answers ("What is the capital gains tax rate for 2026?")
- Questions requiring synthesis from multiple sources ("What are the pros and cons of heat pumps vs. traditional furnaces?")
- "How do I" questions ("How do I dispute a charge on my credit card?")
- Comparison questions ("Which streaming service has the best selection of documentaries?")
- Current events questions ("What happened at today's Senate hearing?")

**The types of searches where Google still has an edge:**

- Navigational searches ("Facebook login," "Amazon")
- Local searches ("pizza delivery near me" — though Perplexity is improving here)
- Shopping with visual browsing ("running shoes under $100")
- Image search when you need to browse many images

Over time, you will develop an instinct for which tool to reach for. Most people find that Perplexity handles 70 to 80 percent of their daily searches better than Google, with the remainder going to Google for local, navigational, and shopping queries.

## Everyday Use Cases

Let's walk through the daily searches where Perplexity shines.

### Cooking and Meal Planning

Instead of browsing recipe websites cluttered with life stories and pop-up ads, ask Perplexity directly:

- "Give me a 30-minute dinner recipe using chicken thighs, sweet potatoes, and broccoli"
- "What substitutions can I make for eggs in banana bread?"

- "How long do I cook a 12-pound turkey and at what temperature?"
- "Plan five weeknight dinners for a family of four on a $75 grocery budget"

Perplexity gives you the information directly — no scrolling past a 2,000-word preamble about someone's grandmother's kitchen to find the recipe.

### Health Questions

For non-emergency health questions, Perplexity provides clear, cited information faster than browsing medical websites:

- "What are the common side effects of metformin?"
- "How long is a cold contagious after symptoms start?"
- "What is the difference between a sprain and a strain?"
- "My child has a 101-degree fever — when should I call the doctor?"

**Important caveat:** Perplexity is excellent for health information but is not a substitute for professional medical advice. Use it to educate yourself and prepare questions for your doctor, not to diagnose or treat conditions on your own.

### Home Maintenance and DIY

The combination of Web and Video Focus modes makes Perplexity a strong assistant for home projects:

- "How do I unclog a garbage disposal safely?"
- "What type of paint should I use for a bathroom ceiling?"
- "My dishwasher is leaving white residue on glasses. What causes this and how do I fix it?"
- "Step-by-step instructions for replacing a light switch"

For anything involving a physical process, switch to Video Focus after the text explanation. Seeing the procedure often beats reading about it.

### Shopping and Purchase Decisions

When you are considering a purchase, Perplexity can save you hours of comparison shopping and review reading:

- "Is the Dyson V15 worth the price compared to mid-range cordless vacuums?"
- "What is the best car seat for a newborn that fits in a Honda Civic?"
- "Compare the top-rated wireless earbuds under $100 for running"
- "What should I look for when buying a used DSLR camera?"

For purchase decisions, combine Web Focus (for professional reviews) with Social Focus (for real-world user experiences). The combination gives you a rounder picture than either alone.

### Travel Planning

Perplexity is an outstanding travel research tool:

- "What is the best time of year to visit Lisbon, Portugal, considering weather and crowds?"
- "What documents do I need to drive a rental car in Japan as an American?"
- "Plan a three-day itinerary for Rome focusing on history and food, avoiding tourist traps"
- "What is the cheapest way to get from the Barcelona airport to the city center?"

Follow-up questions are particularly valuable for travel planning. Start broad, then drill down: "Tell me more about that neighborhood. What restaurants do you recommend there? What is the public transit situation?"

### Parenting and Family

Parents search the internet constantly, and most of those searches are time-sensitive — you need an answer now, not after five articles:

- "Is it normal for a 2-year-old to not be speaking in full sentences yet?"
- "What are age-appropriate chores for a 7-year-old?"
- "How do I explain death to a 4-year-old?"
- "What is the current recommendation for screen time for elementary school children?"

### Personal Finance

For financial questions that do not require professional advice:

- "How much should I contribute to my 401k to get the full employer match?"
- "What is the penalty for early withdrawal from a traditional IRA?"
- "Explain the difference between a traditional and Roth 401k in simple terms"
- "What are the current interest rates for 30-year fixed mortgages?"

For deeper financial analysis, switch to Finance Focus mode.

## Productivity Workflows

Beyond answering individual questions, Perplexity streamlines several common productivity tasks.

### Email Drafting

Use Writing Focus mode to draft emails faster:

- "Write a professional email to my landlord requesting maintenance for a broken dishwasher"
- "Draft a polite email declining a party invitation because of a scheduling conflict"
- "Help me write a follow-up email after a job interview for a marketing manager position"

Paste the output into your email client and edit as needed. Even if you change 50 percent of the draft, you save time by not starting from a blank page.

### Summarizing Information

When you encounter a long article, report, or document:

- Paste the URL and ask "Summarize the key points of this article"
- Upload a PDF and ask "What are the main findings and recommendations?"

- Share a lengthy email thread and ask "What are the key decisions and action items from this conversation?"

### Learning New Skills

Perplexity excels as a learning companion:

- "I want to learn basic Python programming. What should I learn first, and what free resources are best?"
- "Explain the basics of personal investing as if I know nothing about finance"
- "What are the fundamental principles of graphic design that a beginner should learn?"

Use follow-ups to deepen your understanding at your own pace. Ask for examples, request clarification on confusing points, and have Perplexity quiz you on what you have learned.

### Fact-Checking

In an era of misinformation, quick fact-checking is a valuable daily habit:

- "Is it true that you lose most of your body heat through your head?"
- "Did [public figure] actually say [quote I saw on social media]?"
- "Is there evidence that [viral health claim] is true?"

Perplexity's citations make it easy to evaluate the evidence behind any claim. If the sources are reputable and consistent, the claim is likely solid. If the citations are weak or conflicting, be skeptical.

## Mobile Workflows

Some of the most valuable Perplexity use cases are mobile-specific, because they happen when you are out in the world and need an answer now.

**At the grocery store:** "Is this ingredient list safe for someone with a tree nut allergy?" (Snap a photo and upload it.)

**At a restaurant:** "What pairs well with lamb tagine – red or white wine, and what variety?"

**In a meeting:** Quick fact-check or background on a topic that just came up. Use the global hotkey or widget for a fast, discreet search.

**While reading:** Hit an unfamiliar term, concept, or reference? Switch to Perplexity for an instant explanation without losing your place.

**While commuting:** Use voice input to ask Perplexity questions hands-free. "What's the traffic situation on I-95 right now and are there alternate routes?"

## Building a Daily Perplexity Habit

The people who get the most value from Perplexity are not the ones who use it for occasional Deep Research. They are the ones who have made it their default information tool — the first place they go for any question.

Here is a simple framework for building that habit:

**Week 1: Awareness.** Use Perplexity for searches you would normally Google. Notice the difference. Note which queries Perplexity handles well and which still send you to Google.

**Week 2: Expansion.** Start using Perplexity for tasks you would not normally search for at all — drafting messages, planning meals, learning concepts, checking facts. Explore what it does beyond answering questions.

**Week 3: Integration.** Set up the Perplexity hotkey, widget, and extension. Make it the easiest search tool to reach for, on every device. Remove friction.

**Week 4: Optimization.** Now that you are using Perplexity regularly, fine-tune your approach. Experiment with different models for different tasks. Try Focus modes you have not explored. Practice crafting better queries.

By the end of a month, Perplexity will feel as natural as Google does today — possibly more so, because you will be getting better answers with less effort.

## When Perplexity Is Not the Right Tool

Honesty about limitations builds trust in a tool's strengths. Here are situations where Perplexity is not your best option:

**Emergency information.** If you need emergency services, call 911 (or your local equivalent). Do not search for help.

**Real-time navigation.** Google Maps, Waze, and Apple Maps are better for turn-by-turn directions and live traffic.

**Social browsing.** If you want to scroll through social media feeds, Perplexity is not the tool. It finds information within social media, but it is not a social media client.

**Highly personal advice.** While Perplexity can inform your decisions, major life choices — medical treatments, legal strategies, financial plans — benefit from professional human advisors who know your specific situation.

**Entertainment search.** Looking for something to watch tonight? Netflix, streaming aggregators, and recommendation engines beat a general search tool.

Knowing when not to use a tool is as important as knowing when to use it. Perplexity handles a wide range of daily searches, but it is not the only tool you need.

In the next chapter, we look at how Perplexity fits into professional and work contexts — where the stakes are higher and the payoff from effective search is even greater.

# Chapter 9: Professional and Work Use

## Perplexity as a Professional Tool

Everything we have covered so far applies whether you are searching out of personal curiosity or professional need. But the professional context raises the stakes. When you are making business decisions, advising clients, preparing reports, or competing in a market, the quality, speed, and reliability of your information directly affect outcomes — revenue, reputation, career advancement, and competitive position.

This chapter is about using Perplexity in professional settings where the margin for error is smaller and the value of good information is higher. We cover workflows for specific professions, team collaboration with Enterprise features, strategies for folding Perplexity into existing work processes, and the data privacy and professional responsibility considerations that come with high-stakes use.

## Why Professionals Need Better Search

Consider how much of professional work is, at its core, information work. A lawyer researching case precedent. A financial analyst evaluating a company's prospects. A marketer studying a competitor's strategy. A consultant preparing for a client engagement. A journalist fact-checking a story. A product manager researching user needs.

All of these tasks start with search — finding, evaluating, and synthesizing information. And in most professional contexts, this search runs on the same consumer tools everyone else uses: Google, maybe some specialized databases, perhaps a ChatGPT subscription. The quality of the search process determines the quality of the professional output, yet most professionals have never been trained in AI-powered research and are still using methods that have not changed in twenty years.

Perplexity changes the equation. Pro Search, Deep Research, Focus modes, file uploads, and model selection give professionals a toolkit that compresses hours of research into minutes — without sacrificing the rigor professional work demands.

## Professional Workflows by Industry

### Business and Strategy

**Market research.** Before launching a product, entering a new market, or making a strategic decision, you need to understand the landscape. Use Deep Research to generate comprehensive market analysis reports. Combine Finance Focus for hard data with Social Focus for market sentiment and Web Focus for competitive intelligence.

Example workflow for evaluating a new market:

1. Deep Research: "Produce a comprehensive analysis of the North American meal kit delivery market, including market size, growth trends, major players, customer demographics, and key challenges."
2. Finance Focus: "What are the financial results and growth metrics for HelloFresh, Blue Apron, and other publicly traded meal kit companies?"
3. Social Focus: "What are the most common complaints and praise from meal kit delivery customers on Reddit and review sites?"
4. Follow-up: "Based on this analysis, what underserved segments or unmet needs exist in this market?"

**Competitive intelligence.** Use Perplexity to monitor what competitors are doing — new product launches, leadership changes, strategic pivots, public statements, and customer reactions. Set up a Space for each major competitor and add new searches over time to build a longitudinal view.

**Meeting preparation.** Before meeting with a prospect, partner, or investor, run a quick Perplexity deep dive. "Summarize [Company]'s recent news, financial performance, leadership team, and strategic priorities." Walk in informed.

### Finance and Investing

Finance Focus mode was built for this context. Use it to access SEC filings, earnings data, analyst reports, and economic indicators without sifting through general news.

**Earnings analysis.** When a company reports earnings, Finance Focus pulls the key numbers, compares them to expectations, and surfaces analyst reactions —

all in one search. Follow up with Social Focus to see what retail investors are saying.

**Due diligence.** For investment due diligence, Deep Research produces comprehensive profiles of target companies, including financial history, competitive position, risk factors, and management track record.

**Economic analysis.** "What are the leading indicators suggesting about the direction of the US economy over the next 12 months?" Use Finance Focus and ask for data-driven answers with specific indicators and current readings.

### Legal

Lawyers have some of the highest information requirements of any profession. While Perplexity does not replace specialized legal databases like Westlaw or LexisNexis, it complements them.

**Initial research.** Before diving into legal databases, use Perplexity to build a general understanding of a legal issue. "What is the current legal landscape around AI-generated content and copyright in the United States?" That orientation search sharpens your queries for specialized tools.

**Plain-language explanation.** Legal concepts are often dense. Use Perplexity to check your understanding: "Explain the doctrine of promissory estoppel in plain language with a practical example."

**Regulatory monitoring.** Use Pro Search to track regulatory developments: "What new federal regulations affecting healthcare data privacy have been proposed or enacted in 2026?"

**Client-facing summaries.** Use Writing Focus to translate legal analysis into language your clients can understand. Upload your technical memo and ask Perplexity to produce a client-friendly summary.

### Healthcare

Healthcare professionals need accurate, evidence-based information, and they need it quickly.

**Clinical queries.** Academic Focus mode searches medical journals and databases: "What does the current evidence say about the efficacy of GLP-1 receptor agonists for weight management in non-diabetic patients?"

**Drug interactions.** "Are there known interactions between metformin and lisinopril?" Academic Focus finds relevant pharmacological studies and clinical guidelines.

**Patient education.** Use Writing Focus to create patient-friendly explanations of diagnoses, procedures, and treatment options.

**Important note:** Perplexity is a research tool, not a clinical decision support system. Clinical decisions should rest on established medical guidelines, patient-specific factors, and professional judgment. Use Perplexity to stay informed, not to replace clinical reasoning.

### Marketing and Communications

**Content research.** Before writing anything — blog posts, white papers, social media campaigns — use Perplexity to research the topic thoroughly. Deep Research produces a comprehensive brief that gives you everything you need to write authoritatively.

**Audience analysis.** Social Focus reveals how your target audience talks about your industry, product category, or brand. "What are the main frustrations people express about [product category] on Reddit and social media?"

**Trend identification.** "What are the emerging trends in B2B content marketing for 2026?" Use Pro Search for thorough analysis, then dive deeper into the most relevant trends.

**Messaging development.** Upload competitor materials and ask Perplexity to analyze their messaging strategy, positioning, and key claims. Use the insights to sharpen your own messaging.

### Education and Academia

**Literature review.** Academic Focus is essential for building literature reviews. "What are the seminal papers on constructivist learning theory, and what are the most significant recent additions to this body of work?"

**Research design.** "What methodological approaches have been used to study the impact of social media on adolescent mental health, and what are the strengths and limitations of each?"

**Grant writing.** Use Perplexity to research funding opportunities, understand funder priorities, and gather evidence to support your proposals.

**Lecture preparation.** Deep Research generates comprehensive topic overviews that serve as the foundation for lecture content. Academic Focus ensures the material is grounded in current scholarship.

## Enterprise Features for Teams

For organizations deploying Perplexity across teams, the Enterprise plans — Enterprise Pro and Enterprise Max — add collaboration and management capabilities that individual plans lack.

### Shared Spaces

The Enterprise feature that pays off most in daily work is Shared Spaces. A team on a project can all contribute to and draw from a single Space. The marketing team researching a product launch, the legal team conducting due diligence, the strategy team evaluating an acquisition — all can work in a shared Space where everyone's research is visible and builds on what others have found.

**Best practices for Shared Spaces:**

- Establish naming conventions so Spaces are easy to find and understand
- Assign a Space owner responsible for organization and cleanup
- Use Spaces for projects with a defined scope, not as general-purpose knowledge dumps
- Periodically review and archive completed Spaces to keep the workspace manageable

### Administrative Controls

Enterprise plans give administrators tools to manage how the organization uses Perplexity:

- **User management.** Add and remove team members, assign roles, manage permissions
- **SSO integration.** Connect Perplexity to your organization's identity provider for seamless and secure authentication
- **Usage analytics.** Understand how your team uses Perplexity — which features, how often, and for what types of queries. This data helps justify the investment and identify training opportunities
- **Data policies.** Configure data retention and handling policies to meet your organization's requirements

### Making the Case for Enterprise

If you are considering Perplexity for your team and need to justify the investment, here is the framework that works:

**Calculate current research time.** Have team members track how much time they spend searching for and synthesizing information over a two-week period. For knowledge workers, this is typically 15 to 25 percent of work hours.

**Estimate time savings.** Even conservative estimates suggest Perplexity reduces research time by 30 to 50 percent for typical professional search tasks. Multiply the time savings by the team's average hourly cost.

**Compare to subscription cost.** Enterprise Pro at $40/seat/month is $480 per year per person. If a professional with a fully loaded cost of $100/hour saves just five hours a month, the ROI is straightforward.

**Add quality benefits.** Faster research also means more thorough research in the same time budget. Better information leads to better decisions, which is harder to quantify but often more valuable than the time savings alone.

## Integrating Perplexity into Existing Workflows

The biggest challenge in adopting any new tool is not learning to use it — it is building the habit of reaching for it at the right moment. Here are strategies for folding Perplexity into existing professional workflows.

### The Research-First Habit

Before starting any significant work task — writing a report, preparing a presentation, making a recommendation, drafting a proposal — spend five minutes in Perplexity on orientation research. Even if you think you know the topic well, a quick search often surfaces new information, recent developments, or perspectives you had not considered.

### The Second-Opinion Workflow

When you have completed analysis using other tools or your own expertise, run the key conclusions through Perplexity as a sanity check. "I have concluded that [your conclusion]. What evidence supports or contradicts this position?" This is not about replacing your judgment — it is about stress-testing it.

### The Preparation Ritual

Before meetings, calls, presentations, or negotiations, spend three to five minutes in Perplexity gathering background. The goal is not deep research — it is making sure you are current and prepared. "What are the latest developments regarding [meeting topic]?" or "Summarize [person/company] recent news and activities."

### The Handoff Workflow

When you complete a research task in Perplexity, use Pages to create a shareable summary. This transforms your research from a personal search history into a deliverable colleagues can reference and build on. It also documents your research process, which matters for teams that need to understand how conclusions were reached.

## Data Privacy and Professional Responsibility

Using AI search tools in a professional context comes with responsibilities that casual personal use does not.

### Sensitive Information

Be thoughtful about what you type into Perplexity. The company has privacy policies and data handling practices, but the general principle for any cloud-based tool applies: do not enter information that would cause harm if it were exposed.

- Do not paste confidential client information into searches unless your organization's data policy permits it
- Do not upload documents containing trade secrets, personally identifiable information, or privileged communications without appropriate authorization
- Be aware that search queries themselves can contain sensitive information — a query like "What are the legal risks of [specific business action our company is considering]?" reveals strategic intent

Enterprise plans offer enhanced data handling controls, which is one reason organizations should prefer Enterprise plans over individual Pro or Max subscriptions for work use.

### Professional Standards

Different professions have different standards for information sourcing. Understand and follow yours:

- **Legal professionals** must verify any legal citation or claim through authoritative legal databases. Perplexity is a starting point, not a primary source for legal authority.
- **Healthcare professionals** should verify clinical information through established medical guidelines and peer-reviewed sources.
- **Financial professionals** should confirm data from primary sources (SEC filings, company reports) rather than relying on AI-synthesized summaries for regulated communications.
- **Journalists** should independently verify claims and contact original sources, using Perplexity for leads and background rather than as a quotable source.

### Disclosure

In some professional contexts, you may need to disclose that AI tools assisted your research or writing. Academic institutions increasingly have policies on AI use. Some industries have regulatory guidance on AI-assisted work products. Know the norms and requirements in your field and comply with them.

## The Future of Professional Search

We are at the start of a major shift in how professionals find and use information. The combination of AI language models and real-time web search is not just a faster way to do what we have always done — it enables new kinds of work that were not practical before.

A consultant who would have spent three days on market research can do it in three hours and spend the rest on higher-value strategic thinking. A lawyer who would have spent a day reviewing regulatory changes can stay current in thirty minutes. A marketer who would have hired an agency for competitive analysis can do it in-house with greater speed and lower cost.

The professionals who thrive in this environment will not be the ones who resist these tools — they will be the ones who master them early and build workflows that pair AI capability with human judgment, creativity, and expertise.

## Chapter Summary

This chapter covered professional applications of Perplexity across industries — business strategy, finance, legal, healthcare, marketing, and academia — along with Enterprise collaboration features and strategies for folding Perplexity into existing workflows. We also addressed the data privacy and professional responsibility considerations that come with using AI search tools in high-stakes work.

The techniques here are a starting point. As you apply them in your own professional setting, you will develop instincts for which combination of models, Focus modes, and research strategies works best for your needs. The goal is not to replace your professional expertise with AI — it is to amplify that expertise by giving you faster, better access to the information you need.

In the next chapter, we take a deep dive into Spaces — Perplexity's collaborative research workspaces that turn the individual workflows we discussed here into team-powered research environments.

# Part IV: Advanced Features

*"The secret of getting ahead is getting started."*

— Mark Twain (attributed)

# Chapter 10: Spaces

## Your Collaborative Research Headquarters

If you have ever juggled a dozen browser tabs, a shared Google Doc, and a group chat just to keep a research project on track, you already understand the problem Perplexity Spaces are designed to solve. Spaces give you a single, persistent workspace where you can organize threads, share context with collaborators, and set custom instructions that shape every answer the AI produces inside that workspace.

Think of a Space as a dedicated research room. You walk in, pin reference materials to the wall, write the ground rules on the whiteboard, invite your teammates, and every conversation that happens in that room follows those rules and draws on those materials. When the project wraps up, the room — and everything in it — stays intact for future reference.

This chapter walks you through creating, configuring, and getting the most out of Spaces, whether you are a solo researcher or part of a large enterprise team.

---

## What Exactly Is a Space?

A Space is a named container that holds:

- **Threads** — individual conversations with Perplexity that share the Space's context and instructions.
- **Custom instructions** — persistent directives that tell Perplexity how to behave inside this Space (tone, formatting, focus areas, constraints).
- **Files** — uploaded documents, PDFs, images, and spreadsheets that Perplexity can reference when answering questions.
- **Collaborators** — other Perplexity users who can view, contribute to, or manage the Space.

Every thread you start inside a Space inherits the custom instructions and has access to the uploaded files. You do not have to repeat yourself every time you open a new conversation. The AI already knows the rules.

---

## Creating Your First Space

Setting up a Space takes about thirty seconds:

1. Open Perplexity and look for the **Spaces** section in the left sidebar.
2. Click **Create a Space** (or the plus icon next to the Spaces heading).
3. Give your Space a descriptive name. "Q2 Market Research," "Thesis Literature Review," or "Product Launch Competitive Analysis" are all better than "Stuff."
4. Optionally add a description so collaborators understand the Space's purpose at a glance.
5. Click **Create**.

You now have an empty Space ready for configuration.

---

## Setting Custom Instructions

Custom instructions are where Spaces become powerful. They let you define persistent behavior that applies to every thread in the Space. A few examples of what you can do:

- **Define a persona**: "You are a senior financial analyst. Cite specific data points and avoid speculative language."
- **Set formatting rules**: "Always respond with bullet points. Include a summary section at the top of every answer."
- **Constrain sources**: "Prioritize peer-reviewed medical journals. Do not cite social media posts or blog articles."
- **Establish terminology**: "Use 'customer' instead of 'user.' Refer to our product as 'Beacon' throughout."

- **Set language preferences**: “Respond in Brazilian Portuguese unless I ask otherwise.”

To add custom instructions:

1. Open your Space.
2. Click the **Settings** or **gear icon**.
3. Find the **Custom Instructions** field.
4. Type your directives. Be specific and clear — the AI follows these literally.
5. Save.

You can update custom instructions at any time. Changes apply to new threads and new messages in existing threads, but they do not retroactively alter previous responses.

### Tips for Writing Effective Custom Instructions

**Be concrete, not vague.** “Be helpful” does nothing — the AI is already trying to be helpful. “Structure every response as a numbered list with no more than seven items” gives the AI something actionable.

**Layer your instructions.** Start with the role or persona, then add formatting rules, then source constraints. The hierarchy makes it easier to update individual parts later.

**Test and iterate.** After setting instructions, run a few test queries. If the output does not match your expectations, refine the wording. Sometimes a small change — “always” instead of “try to” — makes a real difference.

**Do not overload.** If your custom instructions run longer than a page, consider whether you are trying to do too much in a single Space. It may be better to split the work across two Spaces with more focused instructions each.

---

## Uploading Files to a Space

You can upload documents directly into a Space so Perplexity can reference them when answering questions. This is particularly useful when you are working with proprietary data, internal reports, or specialized reference material that would not surface in a web search.

Supported file types include PDFs, Word documents, text files, spreadsheets, and images. To upload:

1. Open your Space.
2. Click the **Add Files** button (or drag and drop files into the Space).
3. Wait for the upload and processing to complete.

Once files are uploaded, you can ask questions about them directly: “Summarize the key findings from the Q3 report I uploaded,” or “Compare the revenue projections in the two spreadsheets.”

### Enterprise File Sync

For enterprise users, Spaces support file sync with cloud storage platforms. Your Space stays up to date with the latest versions of documents stored in services like Google Drive, SharePoint, Dropbox, OneDrive, and Box. When someone updates a file in the connected cloud folder, the Space picks up the changes automatically. That is a significant advantage for teams working with living documents — you never have to remember to re-upload a revised version.

---

## Collaborating with Others

Spaces are built for teamwork. You can invite collaborators by email or username, and each one can be assigned a role:

- **Viewer** — can read threads and files but cannot create new ones.
- **Contributor** — can start threads, upload files, and participate in conversations.
- **Admin** — can do everything a contributor can, plus edit custom instructions, manage members, and delete the Space.

To invite collaborators:

1. Open your Space and go to **Settings** or **Members**.
2. Click **Invite**.

3. Enter the person's email address or Perplexity username.
4. Assign a role.
5. Send the invitation.

Collaborators see the same threads, files, and custom instructions. When one person starts a thread and gets useful results, everyone in the Space benefits.

### Best Practices for Team Spaces

**Agree on naming conventions.** If everyone names threads descriptively — "Competitor pricing analysis: Acme Corp" rather than "Quick question" — the Space stays navigable even after dozens of threads accumulate.

**Use the description field.** A one-sentence description of the Space's purpose saves new collaborators from having to ask what the Space is for.

**Review custom instructions as a team.** When multiple people rely on the same Space, make sure everyone agrees on the instructions. A directive that makes sense to the person who wrote it might confuse others — or produce unexpected results for someone with a different mental model.

**Archive completed Spaces.** When a project wraps up, do not delete the Space. Archive it so the research stays accessible. You might need it six months later.

---

## Practical Use Cases

### Academic Research

Create a Space for your thesis or dissertation. Upload your literature review PDFs, set custom instructions to prioritize academic sources and formal language, and invite your advisor as a viewer. Every thread you start — whether exploring a subtopic, drafting a section outline, or fact-checking a claim — benefits from the same curated context.

### Product Development

A product team might create a Space called "Competitive Landscape 2026" with instructions to focus on the B2B SaaS market, uploaded competitor reports, and formatting rules that produce comparison tables. Anyone on the team can start a thread to investigate a specific competitor or feature category, and the Space keeps the research consistent.

### Content Creation

If you run a blog or newsletter, set up a Space with your style guide as a custom instruction. Upload past articles as reference material. Every time you start a new thread to research a topic or draft an outline, the AI already knows your voice, audience, and formatting preferences.

### Legal Research

Lawyers and paralegals can upload case documents, set instructions to cite specific jurisdictions and use precise legal terminology, and collaborate with colleagues on complex matters. The Space keeps everything organized and stops the AI from wandering into irrelevant territory.

### Personal Knowledge Management

You do not need a team to benefit from Spaces. Create a personal Space for a topic you care about — say, astrophysics or urban planning. Upload key papers, set instructions that match your expertise, and use the Space as an ongoing research companion. Over time, the collection of threads becomes a searchable archive of your exploration.

---

## Spaces vs. Regular Threads

You might wonder when to use a Space versus a standalone thread. The call is straightforward:

- **Use a regular thread** when you have a quick, one-off question that does not need special context or instructions. "What time does the pharmacy close?" does not need a Space.
- **Use a Space** when you have an ongoing project, need consistent formatting or behavior, want to share research with others, or are working with uploaded documents.

The overhead of creating a Space is minimal, so when in doubt, create one. Start with a single thread inside it and expand later.

---

## Managing and Organizing Spaces

As you use Perplexity more, you will accumulate Spaces. A few habits keep things manageable:

- **Name Spaces by project, not by date.** "Website Redesign" is easier to find than "March Research."
- **Pin frequently used Spaces** to the top of your sidebar for quick access.
- **Delete or archive Spaces** you no longer need. A cluttered sidebar slows you down.
- **Review custom instructions periodically** in long-running Spaces. Your needs evolve, and instructions that made sense three months ago may need updating.

---

## Limitations to Keep in Mind

Spaces are powerful, not magic. A few things to be aware of:

- **Custom instructions have a character limit.** You cannot paste an entire style guide into the instructions field. Summarize the key points and upload the full document as a file instead.
- **File processing is not instant.** Large PDFs or complex spreadsheets take time to index. Give the system a moment before querying uploaded documents.
- **Collaborator changes propagate immediately.** If an admin changes the custom instructions, every new response in every thread reflects the change. Communicate with your team before making significant adjustments.
- **Spaces do not replace a database.** If you need to store and query thousands of documents, Spaces are not the right tool. They are built for curated collections of reference material, not massive data warehouses.

## Chapter Summary

Spaces turn Perplexity from a search tool into a research platform. By combining persistent custom instructions, file uploads, and collaboration, Spaces let you build dedicated environments for any project — academic, professional, or personal. The key is thoughtful setup: clear instructions, descriptive names, and organized files. Once the foundation is in place, every conversation in that Space benefits automatically.

In the next chapter, you will learn about Pages — Perplexity's tool for turning your research into polished, shareable reports.

# Chapter 11: Pages

## Turning Research into Shareable Reports

You have done the research. You have asked the right questions, followed up with clarifying queries, and arrived at a solid understanding of your topic. Now what? If you are like most people, you copy key passages into a document, reformat everything, add headings, and spend almost as long organizing the output as you did generating it.

Pages eliminate that step. They take your Perplexity research and transform it into a structured, polished, shareable report — complete with sections, citations, and a table of contents — in seconds.

This chapter covers what Pages are, when to use them, how to create and customize them, and how to share them.

---

## What Is a Page?

A Page is a structured document Perplexity generates from your research. Unlike a thread — a back-and-forth conversation — a Page is a standalone, readable article. It has:

- **A title and introduction** that frame the topic.
- **Organized sections** with headings and subheadings.
- **Inline citations** linking back to the sources Perplexity used.
- **A clean, readable layout** designed for sharing.

Think of it as the difference between your raw interview notes and the finished magazine article. The thread is the notes; the Page is the article.

---

## When to Use Pages

Pages shine when you need to communicate your findings to someone else — or to your future self. Common scenarios:

- **Briefing documents** for a manager or client who does not want to read through a dozen thread messages.
- **Research summaries** for a class assignment or team meeting.
- **Topic overviews** you want to bookmark and revisit later.
- **Shareable explainers** you can send to a colleague, post on social media, or embed in a presentation.
- **Quick reference guides** on a subject you are learning.

If you are the only person who will see the output and you do not need it organized, a regular thread is fine. But the moment you want structure, polish, or shareability, reach for Pages.

---

## Creating a Page

There are two main paths to creating a Page:

### Starting from Scratch

1. Look for the **Pages** option in the Perplexity interface (often accessible from the sidebar or the "Create" menu).
2. Enter your topic or question. This can be broad ("The history of renewable energy policy in the EU") or narrow ("Comparing lithium-ion and solid-state battery performance metrics in 2025–2026").
3. Perplexity generates a structured outline, then fills in each section with researched content.
4. Review the output and edit as needed.

### Converting from a Thread

If you have already done research in a thread and want to turn it into a Page:

1. Open the thread with the research you want to use.

2. Look for the **Create Page** or **Generate Page** option.
3. Perplexity analyzes the thread and organizes it into a structured document.
4. Review and edit.

The conversion approach is especially useful when you started with casual exploration and ended up with something worth formalizing.

---

## Customizing Your Page

Once a Page is generated, you are not stuck with the default output. You have several ways to shape the final product:

### Editing Sections

Click into any section to edit the text directly. Rewrite sentences, add your own commentary, remove irrelevant paragraphs, or rearrange the order of sections. The Page is your document — Perplexity generated the first draft, but you own the final version.

### Adjusting the Structure

If the AI organized the content in a way that does not match your needs, you can:

- **Add sections** for topics the AI missed.
- **Remove sections** irrelevant to your audience.
- **Merge sections** that overlap.
- **Reorder sections** to match your preferred narrative flow.

### Controlling Tone and Depth

When you create a Page, you can shape the output with instructions like:

- "Write this for a technical audience familiar with machine learning."
- "Keep the language simple — this is for high school students."
- "Focus on practical applications rather than theory."
- "Include specific numbers and statistics wherever possible."

These instructions shape the entire Page, not just one section.

### Adding Visuals

Pages can incorporate visuals where relevant. If your research involves data, charts, or diagrams, you can ask Perplexity to include them or add your own after the Page is generated.

---

## Citations and Sources

One of the strongest features of Pages is inline citation. Every claim drawn from a web source includes a linked reference, so readers can verify the information or dig deeper.

This matters for several reasons:

- **Credibility.** A report with citations looks and feels more trustworthy than one without.
- **Transparency.** Your readers see exactly where the information came from.
- **Accountability.** If a source turns out to be wrong or outdated, you can trace the claim back and correct it.

When reviewing a Page, always spot-check a few citations to confirm they support the claims they are attached to. The AI is generally accurate, but not infallible. A quick verification pass takes five minutes and can save you from sharing something incorrect.

---

## Sharing Your Page

Once your Page is ready, you have several sharing options:

- **Public link** — generate a shareable URL anyone can access without a Perplexity account.
- **Direct share** — send the Page to specific people via email or messaging.
- **Embed** — in some cases, you can embed a Page in a website or blog.

- **Export** — copy the content into another format (like a Word document or PDF) for distribution through other channels.

The public link option is particularly useful for knowledge sharing. If you create a comprehensive overview of a topic, that link becomes a living resource you can drop into Slack channels, email newsletters, social media posts, or team wikis.

---

## Pages vs. Other Output Formats

You might wonder how Pages compare to other ways of getting information out of Perplexity. Here is a quick comparison:

**Pages vs. Threads.** A thread is a conversation; a Page is a document. Threads are for exploration and follow-up questions. Pages are for presentation and sharing. Use threads for the journey, Pages for the destination.

**Pages vs. Deep Research.** Deep Research (covered in the next chapter) is a more intensive investigation process that produces longer, more detailed reports, presentations, and even dashboards. Pages are lighter and faster — ideal for topics that do not require multi-step investigation. If you need a quick briefing, use a Page. If you need an exhaustive analysis, use Deep Research.

**Pages vs. Copy-Paste.** You can always copy text from a thread and paste it into a Google Doc. But you lose the citations, formatting, and structure. Pages preserve all of that with zero manual effort.

---

## Practical Examples

### Example 1: Meeting Prep

You have a meeting tomorrow with a potential partner company. Create a Page on "Overview of [Company Name]: products, recent news, financial performance, and key leadership." Five minutes later, you have a polished one-pager to review on the way to the meeting or share with your team beforehand.

### Example 2: Student Research Paper

You are writing a paper on the economic impact of remote work. Start with a few threads to explore subtopics — productivity data, real estate market effects, urban-rural migration patterns. Then create a Page that synthesizes the findings into a structured overview with citations. Use that Page as the backbone of your paper.

### Example 3: Newsletter Content

You write a weekly newsletter about AI developments. Each week, create a Page summarizing the most significant news and research from the past seven days. The structured format, complete with citations, gives you a ready-to-publish draft that needs only your editorial voice layered on top.

### Example 4: Client Deliverable

A client asks you to summarize the competitive landscape in their industry. Create a Page with sections for each major competitor, their strengths and weaknesses, recent moves, and market positioning. Share the link directly with the client or export it as a PDF.

---

## Tips for Better Pages

**Start with a clear, specific topic.** "Artificial intelligence" is too broad. "How AI is changing drug discovery timelines in 2025–2026" gives Perplexity something concrete to research and organize.

**Use thread research as input.** If you have already explored a topic in a thread, convert it to a Page rather than starting from scratch. The thread gives the AI more context to work with.

**Edit ruthlessly.** The AI-generated first draft is a starting point, not a finished product. Cut filler, tighten language, and add your own insights. The best Pages combine AI research efficiency with human editorial judgment.

**Check the citations.** Not every citation will be a perfect source. Some link to paywalled articles, some are tangential, and a few may not fully support the claim. A quick review pass ensures quality.

**Think about your audience.** A Page for your engineering team should read differently from a Page for your board of directors. Adjust the instructions accordingly.

---

## Limitations

Pages are not a replacement for deep, original analysis. They excel at synthesizing existing information into a readable format, but they cannot:

- Generate novel insights that do not exist in the source material.
- Replace domain expertise on highly specialized topics.
- Guarantee that every source is current — some citations may reference older data.
- Produce publication-ready academic papers (though they are a solid starting point for one).

Use Pages as an accelerator, not a replacement, for your own thinking.

---

## Chapter Summary

Pages turn your Perplexity research into structured, citation-rich, shareable documents. They are ideal for briefings, summaries, and reports that need to communicate findings clearly. The workflow is simple: research in threads, generate a Page, customize and edit, then share. The result is a polished output that would have taken much longer to produce manually.

Next up, we tackle Deep Research — Perplexity's most powerful investigation tool, capable of producing not just reports but presentations, spreadsheets, dashboards, and even websites.

# Chapter 12: Deep Research

## When You Need More Than a Quick Answer

Sometimes a single search query is not enough. You need an answer that draws on dozens of sources, follows a chain of reasoning through multiple steps, weighs conflicting evidence, and delivers a comprehensive analysis. Deep Research was built for this.

Deep Research is Perplexity's most powerful investigation mode. Instead of returning a quick response based on a handful of sources, it runs a multi-step process: planning an investigation strategy, executing searches across multiple angles, synthesizing findings, and producing a detailed output. The output is not limited to text. Deep Research can generate presentations, spreadsheets, dashboards, and even functional websites.

This chapter explains how Deep Research works, when to use it, and how to get the best results from it.

---

## How Deep Research Works

When you activate Deep Research, Perplexity does not just run one search and summarize the results. It follows a multi-step process that resembles how a skilled human researcher would approach a complex question:

1. **Planning.** The system analyzes your query and breaks it down into sub-questions. If you ask "What are the economic, environmental, and social implications of large-scale desalination in the Middle East?", it identifies that it needs to investigate economics, environmental impact, and social factors as separate threads of inquiry.

2. **Searching.** It runs multiple searches, each targeting a different aspect of your question. It does not stop at the first page of results — it digs deeper, following leads from one source to the next.

3. **Reading and analyzing.** Deep Research reads the sources it finds, extracting relevant data points, identifying contradictions, and noting gaps in the available information.
4. **Synthesizing.** It combines findings from all its sub-investigations into a coherent analysis, organizing the information logically and flagging areas where evidence conflicts or is insufficient.
5. **Producing output.** The final result is a structured report, often several pages long, with citations throughout. Depending on your request, it may also produce supplementary outputs like charts, tables, or other formats.

You can watch this unfold in real time. Perplexity shows you what it is searching for, which sources it is examining, and how it is building its analysis. The transparency matters — it lets you course-correct if the research is heading in the wrong direction.

---

## Activating Deep Research

Using Deep Research is straightforward:

1. Start a new query in Perplexity.
2. Before submitting, look for the **Deep Research** toggle or option. It may appear as a button near the search bar, a dropdown selection, or a toggle switch depending on your interface.
3. Enable it and submit your query.
4. Wait. Deep Research takes longer than a standard query — sometimes a few minutes for complex topics. That is normal. The system is doing significantly more work.

Deep Research is available to Pro and Max subscribers. The free tier does not include it.

---

## What Deep Research Can Produce

Here is where Deep Research separates itself from other search tools. The output is not limited to a text report. Depending on your query and instructions, Deep Research can generate:

### Detailed Reports

The default output is a long-form, structured report with sections, subsections, citations, and analysis. These reports typically run several pages and go deeper than a standard Perplexity response. They suit academic research, business intelligence, due diligence, and policy analysis.

### Presentations

Ask Deep Research to produce a presentation on your topic and it generates slide-by-slide content with titles, bullet points, and speaker notes. This is not a rough outline — it is a presentation-ready structure that you can refine and drop into your preferred slide tool.

### Spreadsheets

For data-heavy queries, Deep Research can organize its findings into spreadsheet format. Comparative analyses, market data, feature matrices, and statistical summaries all translate well into rows and columns. You get structured data you can sort, filter, and work with immediately.

### Dashboards

For certain analytical queries, Deep Research can produce interactive dashboard-style outputs that visualize data and relationships. Useful for business intelligence, market analysis, and any scenario where you need to see patterns at a glance rather than read through paragraphs of text.

### Websites

Perhaps the most surprising capability: Deep Research can generate functional web pages that present your findings in an interactive, navigable format. Useful for shareable research portals, internal knowledge bases, or client-facing deliverables that go beyond a static document.

## Crafting Effective Deep Research Queries

The quality of your Deep Research output depends heavily on the quality of your input. Here are the principles that make the difference:

### Be Specific About Scope

"Tell me about electric vehicles" produces a sprawling, unfocused report. "Compare the total cost of ownership for the top five electric SUVs available in North America as of early 2026, including purchase price, charging costs, maintenance, insurance, and projected resale value" gives Deep Research a clear mandate.

### Specify the Output Format

If you want a presentation, say so. If you want a comparative spreadsheet, say so. If you want a text report with an executive summary, say so. Deep Research can produce multiple formats, but it needs to know what you want.

### Define Your Audience

"Write this for a board of directors who are not technical" produces a different report than "Write this for a senior engineering team evaluating implementation options." Audience shapes the vocabulary, depth, and focus of the output.

### Set Constraints

If there are specific requirements your output must meet, state them upfront:

- "Limit the analysis to peer-reviewed sources published after 2023."
- "Focus on the European market only."
- "Include a section on regulatory risks."
- "Do not exceed 3,000 words."

Constraints give Deep Research guardrails that improve the relevance of the output.

### Ask for What Is Missing

One of the most underused prompting strategies for Deep Research is asking it to identify gaps: “After completing the analysis, include a section on what data was unavailable, what questions remain unanswered, and what additional research would be needed to reach a definitive conclusion.” That turns Deep Research into an honest advisor rather than a confident summarizer.

---

## Real-World Use Cases

### Due Diligence

Before investing in a company, acquiring a business, or entering a partnership, you need to understand the entity thoroughly. Deep Research can investigate a company’s financial history, legal issues, competitive positioning, leadership team, and public reputation across dozens of sources. The output is a structured report with citations you can verify.

### Market Analysis

Product managers, strategists, and entrepreneurs use Deep Research to map competitive landscapes, identify market trends, and quantify opportunities. A query like “Analyze the North American meal kit delivery market: key players, market size, growth trends, customer demographics, and emerging threats from grocery delivery services” produces a report that would take a human analyst days to compile.

### Academic Literature Reviews

Graduate students and researchers can use Deep Research to survey a field, identify key papers and debates, and map the intellectual landscape of a topic. It cannot replace reading the primary sources yourself, but it accelerates the discovery phase and helps you identify which papers deserve close reading.

### Policy Analysis

Think tanks, government agencies, and advocacy organizations use Deep Research to investigate policy questions with multiple dimensions. “Analyze the potential impact of a four-day work week on productivity, employee wellbeing, business costs, and GDP in OECD countries, drawing on pilot program data from 2020–2026" is exactly the kind of multi-faceted question Deep Research handles well.

### Technical Evaluation

Engineering teams evaluating new technologies, frameworks, or tools can use Deep Research to produce comprehensive comparison reports. Instead of having team members investigate different options separately and reconciling their findings in a meeting, Deep Research produces a unified analysis covering all options against the same criteria.

---

## Reviewing and Refining Deep Research Output

Deep Research is powerful, but never treat its output as final without review. Here is a practical workflow:

1. **Read the executive summary or introduction first.** Does it accurately frame the question? Does it cover all the dimensions you care about?
2. **Scan the section headings.** Is the structure logical? Are there obvious gaps — topics you expected to see covered that are missing?
3. **Spot-check citations.** Pick three to five claims central to the analysis and verify the cited sources. Do the sources actually say what the report claims?
4. **Look for hedging language.** Where does the report say "may," "some evidence suggests," or "it is unclear"? Those phrases mark areas where the evidence is thin. Decide whether you need more certainty before acting on those points.
5. **Check for recency.** Are the sources current enough for your purposes? A market analysis citing data from 2022 may not reflect 2026 conditions.

6. **Follow up.** If the initial report has gaps or raises new questions, ask follow-ups within the same thread. Deep Research builds on its existing analysis rather than starting over.

---

## Deep Research vs. Pages

Both Deep Research and Pages produce structured output, so it is worth clarifying when to use each:

| Feature | Pages | Deep Research |
|---|---|---|
| Speed | Fast (seconds to a minute) | Slower (minutes) |
| Depth | Good overview | Thorough investigation |
| Sources consulted | Moderate | Extensive |
| Output formats | Text report | Reports, presentations, spreadsheets, dashboards, websites |
| Best for | Quick summaries and briefings | Complex, multi-dimensional questions |
| Suitable for decision-making | Background information | Substantive analysis |

Use Pages when you need a quick, organized summary. Use Deep Research when the stakes are higher and the question is more complex.

---

## Cost and Access

Deep Research consumes more computational resources than standard queries, which is why it is limited to Pro and Max subscribers. Within those tiers, there may be daily or monthly limits on the number of Deep Research queries you can run. Check your plan details for specifics.

Given the resource cost, use Deep Research strategically. Do not use it for questions that a standard search or a Page would handle. Reserve it for investigations where thoroughness matters.

## Limitations

Deep Research is impressive, but it is not omniscient:

- **It cannot access paywalled content.** If the best analysis of your topic lives behind a subscription wall, Deep Research cannot read it. You may need to supplement its findings with sources you have access to.
- **It can be overconfident.** Like all AI systems, Deep Research sometimes presents uncertain conclusions with more confidence than warranted. The review process above helps catch this.
- **It takes time.** If you need an answer in thirty seconds, Deep Research is the wrong tool. Plan ahead.
- **Complex quantitative analysis has limits.** Deep Research can find and organize data, but it is not a substitute for a statistician or financial modeler when rigorous quantitative analysis is required.
- **It reflects what is published online.** If your topic involves proprietary data, insider knowledge, or recent events not yet covered by online sources, Deep Research will have blind spots.

## Chapter Summary

Deep Research is Perplexity's most thorough investigation tool. It breaks complex questions into sub-investigations, searches extensively, synthesizes findings, and produces outputs in multiple formats — reports, presentations, spreadsheets, dashboards, and websites. The key to great results is writing specific, well-scoped queries with clear audience and format instructions. Review the output before relying on it for decisions, and use Deep Research for questions that require depth.

In the next chapter, we will look at file uploads and document analysis — how to feed Perplexity your own documents and get intelligent analysis back.

# Chapter 13: File Uploads and Document Analysis

## Making Perplexity Work with Your Documents

Perplexity is excellent at searching the open web. But some of the most valuable information you work with every day does not live on the internet. It lives in the PDF your client sent, the spreadsheet your finance team maintains, the Word document your colleague drafted, or the scanned invoice sitting in your downloads folder.

File uploads bridge the gap. When you upload a document to Perplexity, you give the AI access to your private data so it can read, summarize, compare, extract, and analyze it — combining the document's contents with web search to deliver answers grounded in both your files and the broader internet.

This chapter covers the types of files you can upload, what you can do with them, and how to get the best results from document analysis.

---

## Supported File Types

Perplexity supports a range of common file formats:

- **PDFs** — research papers, reports, legal documents, invoices, manuals, ebooks.
- **Word documents (.docx)** — drafts, memos, proposals, contracts.
- **Text files (.txt)** — notes, logs, plain-text data.
- **Spreadsheets (.csv, .xlsx)** — financial data, survey results, inventory lists, analytics exports.
- **Images (.jpg, .png, .webp)** — photos, screenshots, diagrams, infographics, scanned documents.

Perplexity processes these files to extract their content. It reads the text in your PDF, parses the rows and columns in your spreadsheet, and uses vision capabilities to interpret images. The file is not just stored — it is understood.

---

## How to Upload a File

Uploading is simple:

1. **In a thread**: Click the attachment or paperclip icon near the message input field. Select your file from your device. The file uploads and processes.
2. **In a Space**: Navigate to the Space's file section and add your file there. It then becomes available to every thread within that Space.
3. **Drag and drop**: In most interfaces, drag a file from your desktop or file explorer directly into the Perplexity window.

Give the system a moment to process the file. Small text documents process almost instantly. Large PDFs or complex spreadsheets may take a few seconds longer.

---

## What You Can Do with Uploaded Files

Once a file is uploaded, the possibilities open up. Here are the most common and useful operations:

### Summarization

The most straightforward use case. Upload a long document and ask:

- "Summarize this report in five bullet points."
- "What are the key takeaways from this paper?"
- "Give me a one-paragraph summary suitable for an executive briefing."

This works equally well for a 50-page research paper and a 3-page memo. You control the length and format of the summary.

### Question Answering

Ask specific questions about the document's contents:

- "What revenue figure does this report cite for Q3?"
- "According to this contract, what are the termination conditions?"
- "What methodology did the authors use in this study?"
- "Does this document mention any risks related to supply chain disruption?"

Perplexity searches the document for relevant passages and answers based on what it finds. If the answer is not in the document, it typically tells you so — or offers to search the web for related information.

### Data Extraction

For structured documents like invoices, forms, or tables within PDFs, you can extract specific data:

- "Extract all the line items and their prices from this invoice."
- "Pull out every date mentioned in this contract."
- "List all the authors and their affiliations from this paper."
- "What are the column headers and first ten rows of data in this spreadsheet?"

Powerful for turning unstructured or semi-structured documents into clean, usable data.

### Comparison

Upload two or more documents and ask Perplexity to compare them:

- "Compare the main arguments in these two papers."
- "What are the key differences between these two contract versions?"
- "Which of these two proposals offers better terms for our company?"
- "Compare the financial projections in these two spreadsheets."

Comparison queries save hours when you would otherwise need to read both documents side by side and manually track differences.

### Analysis and Critique

Go beyond summarization by asking for analytical assessment:

- "What are the strengths and weaknesses of the methodology in this paper?"
- "Are there any logical gaps in this proposal?"
- "Does this report's conclusion follow from the data presented?"
- "What questions should I ask the author of this memo?"

This turns Perplexity into a thinking partner, not just a summarizer.

### Translation and Reformatting

If your document is in a language you do not read fluently, Perplexity can translate it. If the format does not suit your needs, ask for reformatting:

- "Translate this French PDF into English."
- "Reformat the data in this spreadsheet as a Markdown table."
- "Convert the key findings in this report into a bulleted list."
- "Rewrite the executive summary of this document for a non-technical audience."

---

## Working with PDFs

PDFs are probably the most commonly uploaded file type, so they deserve special attention.

### Text-Based PDFs

Most modern PDFs contain selectable text. Perplexity handles these well — reading every page, locating specific sections, and quoting directly from the document. You get accurate, reliable results.

### Scanned PDFs

Scanned PDFs — where the pages are essentially images of printed text — are trickier. Perplexity uses OCR to read these, but results depend on the scan quality.

A clean, high-resolution scan of a typed document works well. A grainy photocopy of a handwritten form might not.

If you are uploading scanned documents and getting poor results, try to obtain a cleaner scan or a text-based version.

### Large PDFs

Very long PDFs (hundreds of pages) may push against processing limits. With a massive document, consider:

- Uploading it to a Space, where it can be indexed once and queried across multiple threads.
- Asking about specific sections rather than requesting a summary of the entire document.
- Splitting the PDF into smaller files if your query only pertains to certain chapters or sections.

---

## Working with Spreadsheets

Spreadsheets are a different beast from text documents. Tips for getting the most out of them:

**Make sure your data has headers.** Perplexity uses column headers to understand what each column represents. A spreadsheet with headers like “Date,” “Revenue,” “Region,” and “Product” is easier to work with than one with unlabeled columns.

**Clean your data before uploading.** Remove merged cells, extraneous formatting, and empty rows or columns. The cleaner the spreadsheet, the better the analysis.

**Be specific.** “Analyze this spreadsheet” is too vague. “What is the average monthly revenue by region for 2025?” gives Perplexity a clear task.

**Ask for calculations.** Perplexity can perform basic statistical operations on your data — sums, averages, counts, min/max values, and comparisons between groups. Not a replacement for Excel or a BI tool, but it handles common analytical questions well.

---

## Working with Images

Image uploads enable a different kind of analysis. You can upload:

- **Screenshots** – "What error message is shown in this screenshot?" or "Explain what this dashboard is displaying."
- **Diagrams and charts** – "Describe the trends shown in this bar chart" or "What does this flowchart depict?"
- **Photos of physical documents** – "Read the text in this photo of a business card" or "What does this handwritten note say?"
- **Infographics** – "Summarize the data presented in this infographic."
- **Product photos** – "What brand and model is this device?" or "Identify the plants in this photo."

Image interpretation varies with complexity. The AI handles clean, well-lit, high-resolution images far better than blurry, dark, or cluttered ones.

---

## Combining File Analysis with Web Search

One of the most powerful aspects of file uploads in Perplexity is combining document analysis with web search in a single query. For example:

- "Based on the revenue figures in this spreadsheet, how does our company compare to the industry average?" (File data + web search for industry benchmarks.)
- "This paper claims that global temperatures rose by 1.5 degrees Celsius since 1900. Is that consistent with the latest IPCC data?" (File claim + web verification.)
- "My contract says the arbitration clause follows New York state law. What are the implications of that?" (File content + web research on legal framework.)

The combination is distinctive. Few other tools blend private document analysis with live web research in a single conversation.

---

## Privacy Considerations

When you upload a file to Perplexity, understand what happens to it:

- Your file is processed to extract its contents and enable analysis.
- Check Perplexity's current privacy policy and terms of service for details on data retention, whether uploaded files are used for model training, and how long files are stored.
- If you are working with sensitive documents — legal, medical, financial, or proprietary business data — make sure you are comfortable with the platform's data handling practices before uploading.
- Enterprise plans typically offer stronger data protection guarantees, including commitments not to use uploaded data for training.

We cover privacy in more detail in Chapter 24. For now, the rule of thumb is: do not upload anything you would not be comfortable with the platform's team potentially having access to, unless you are on an enterprise plan with explicit data protection terms.

---

## Best Practices

**Upload the right file.** If you have both a draft and a final version, upload the one you want analyzed.

**Name your files descriptively.** "Q3-2025-Revenue-Report.pdf" is easier to reference in conversation than "Document1.pdf."

**One file per topic when possible.** If you need to compare two documents, upload both. But upload ten unrelated files with a vague question and the AI will struggle to give you a focused answer.

**Reference the file explicitly.** Make it clear you are asking about the uploaded file: "Based on the document I just uploaded..." or "In the attached spreadsheet..."

This prevents Perplexity from defaulting to web search when you want file-based analysis.

**Iterate.** If the first answer is not quite what you need, follow up. "That summary is too detailed. Give me three sentences." Or "You missed the section on risk factors. Please include that."

---

## Limitations

- **File size limits exist.** Very large files may fail to upload or may not be fully processed. Check current limits in Perplexity's documentation.
- **Complex formatting may be lost.** Heavily formatted documents — with nested tables, embedded images, and custom layouts — may not be fully captured during processing. The text gets extracted, but the visual structure may not be preserved.
- **Handwriting recognition is imperfect.** Photos of handwritten text work best when the handwriting is clear and the image is well-lit.
- **Spreadsheet formulas are not executed.** Perplexity reads the data in your spreadsheet but does not run Excel formulas. If your spreadsheet depends on calculated fields, export the calculated values before uploading.

---

## Chapter Summary

File uploads transform Perplexity from a web-only search tool into a personal document analyst. You can upload PDFs, Word documents, spreadsheets, and images, then summarize, query, compare, extract, and analyze their contents. Combining file analysis with web search in a single conversation is a distinctive advantage. Be thoughtful about privacy with sensitive documents, and follow the best practices above for the most useful results.

Next, we explore another visual dimension of Perplexity: image generation and visual features.

# Chapter 14: Image Generation and Visual Features

## Creating and Understanding Images with Perplexity

Perplexity started as a text-first search engine. You typed a question, you got a text answer with citations. The platform has expanded well beyond text. Today, Perplexity can both understand images you provide and generate new images from your descriptions.

This chapter covers both sides: using Perplexity to analyze and interpret images, and using it to create new ones.

---

## Image Understanding

We touched on image uploads in the previous chapter, but image understanding deserves its own spotlight given how broadly useful it is.

When you upload an image to Perplexity, the AI applies vision capabilities to interpret what it sees. This is not simple pattern matching — it involves understanding objects, text, layout, context, and relationships within the image.

### What You Can Ask About an Image

The range of useful queries is wider than most people expect:

**Identification.** "What species of bird is in this photo?" "What architectural style is this building?" "What brand of watch is this?" The AI identifies objects, species, products, landmarks, and more.

**Text extraction.** "Read the text in this photo." "What does this sign say?" "Extract the data from this chart." If there is readable text in the image, Perplexity pulls it out.

**Description.** "Describe this image in detail." "What is happening in this photo?" Useful for accessibility, documentation, or when you need a text description of a visual.

**Explanation.** "Explain the diagram in this image." "What does this error message mean?" "Walk me through this flowchart." The AI interprets structured visual information and explains it in plain language.

**Comparison.** Upload two images and ask, "What are the differences between these two designs?" or "Which of these two rooms has better lighting?"

**Context and research.** "Where was this photo likely taken?" "What era does this furniture belong to?" "What is the historical significance of the monument in this image?" The AI combines what it sees with its knowledge base to provide context.

### Tips for Better Image Analysis

**Use high-resolution images.** The clearer the image, the more accurate the analysis. A blurry photo of a distant sign yields worse results than a crisp close-up.

**Crop to what matters.** If you want Perplexity to analyze a specific element in a busy image, crop to focus on that element before uploading.

**Ask specific questions.** "Tell me about this image" gets a generic description. "What type of rock formation is visible in the foreground of this image?" gets a targeted, useful answer.

**Combine with web search.** After the AI identifies something in your image, ask follow-up questions that draw on web sources. "You identified this as a Romanesque church. What are the key characteristics of Romanesque architecture, and which famous examples should I visit in southern France?"

---

## Image Generation

Image generation is available to Perplexity Pro and Max subscribers. It creates original images from text descriptions directly within the Perplexity interface — no need to switch to a separate AI art tool.

### How It Works

Type a description of the image you want and Perplexity generates it. The description — often called a "prompt" in AI image generation — should be specific enough to guide the output but leave room for creative interpretation.

### Crafting Good Image Prompts

The quality of generated images depends heavily on the quality of your prompt. The principles that matter:

**Describe the subject clearly.** "A dog" is a starting point. "A golden retriever puppy sitting in a field of wildflowers, looking directly at the camera" is far more likely to produce what you envision.

**Specify the style.** Without style guidance, the AI defaults to a generic photorealistic look. If you want something different, say so:

- "In the style of a watercolor painting"
- "As a minimalist line drawing"
- "Photorealistic, shot on a 35mm lens"
- "In the style of a vintage travel poster"
- "As a technical illustration with labeled parts"
- "In the style of a pixel art video game"

**Include context and setting.** "A coffee shop" is vague. "A cozy coffee shop in autumn, warm lighting, exposed brick walls, rain visible through the window, a single steaming cup on a wooden table" creates a scene.

**Specify composition when it matters.** If you need a specific layout — "centered portrait," "wide landscape shot," "close-up detail," "aerial view" — include it in the prompt.

**Mention lighting and mood.** "Bright, high-key lighting" produces a different image than "dramatic shadows, film noir lighting" or "soft golden hour sunlight."

### Practical Uses for Image Generation

Image generation is not just for art. It has a range of practical applications:

**Content creation.** Blog headers, social media graphics, newsletter illustrations, presentation visuals. Instead of hunting through stock photo sites, describe what you need.

**Concept visualization.** "Show me what a rooftop garden on a modern office building might look like" or "Generate an image of an open-plan office with biophilic design elements." Useful for brainstorming, pitching ideas, and early-stage design exploration.

**Education.** "Create a diagram showing the water cycle" or "Generate an illustration of a medieval castle's defensive features with labels." Visual aids make explanations clearer.

**Prototyping.** "Generate a mockup of a mobile app screen for a fitness tracker, showing a daily step count dashboard with a circular progress indicator." Rough prototyping, not production design, but fast and useful for early discussions.

**Storytelling.** Authors, game designers, and content creators use image generation to visualize characters, settings, and scenes. "A cyberpunk street market at night, neon signs in Japanese and English, vendors selling street food, light rain, reflections on wet pavement."

### What Image Generation Cannot Do

Be realistic about the limitations:

- **Consistent characters.** Generating the same character across multiple images is difficult. Faces, clothing details, and body proportions may shift between generations.
- **Precise text in images.** AI image generators struggle with rendering specific text. Letters may come out distorted, misspelled, or nonsensical.
- **Exact reproductions.** If you need an image that precisely matches a detailed specification (specific logo placement, exact color codes, pixel-perfect layouts), use proper design software.
- **Copyrighted material.** Do not use image generation to replicate copyrighted artwork, real people's likenesses, or trademarked logos.
- **Technical accuracy.** Generated images of complex technical subjects (circuit boards, anatomical details, mechanical systems) may look plausible but contain errors an expert would catch.

### Iterating on Generated Images

Your first generated image is rarely perfect. Use an iterative approach:

1. Generate the initial image with your best prompt.
2. Evaluate what works and what does not.
3. Refine your prompt. If the lighting is wrong, add lighting instructions. If the composition is off, specify the layout. If the style is not right, adjust the style descriptors.
4. Generate again.
5. Repeat until you are satisfied.

Each iteration teaches you something about how the model interprets language. Over time, you develop an intuition for prompts that produce better results on the first try.

---

## Visual Search

Beyond generating and analyzing single images, Perplexity supports visual search — using an image as a search query. Instead of describing what you see in words, you show the AI the image and let it find related information.

Useful for:

- **Shopping.** See a piece of furniture you like? Upload a photo and ask, "Where can I buy something like this?"
- **Identification.** Photograph a plant, insect, or mushroom and ask, "What is this?"
- **Research.** Upload a photo of a painting in a museum and ask, "Who painted this, when, and what is its significance?"
- **Troubleshooting.** Upload a photo of a device showing an error indicator and ask, "What does this status light pattern mean?"

---

## Combining Visual and Text Features

The most powerful workflows combine image understanding, image generation, and text-based research:

**Research to visualization.** Research a topic in text, then generate an image to illustrate your findings. "I just learned about Art Deco architecture in Miami Beach. Generate an image that captures the typical features of that style."

**Image to research.** Upload a photo of something you encountered, identify it, then research it deeply. Upload a photo of a building, learn it is Brutalist architecture, then ask for a deep dive into the Brutalist movement.

**Iterative design.** Describe a concept, generate a visual, critique it, refine the prompt, generate again. Useful for creative professionals exploring ideas.

**Document to visual.** Upload a spreadsheet with data, ask Perplexity to summarize the trends, then ask it to generate a visual that represents those trends — either as a chart description or a conceptual illustration.

---

## Best Practices

**Know when to use image generation vs. stock photos vs. professional design.** Image generation is great for quick, custom visuals. Stock photos are better when you need photographic authenticity. Professional design tools are necessary when you need pixel-perfect, brand-consistent output.

**Review generated images before sharing.** Check for visual artifacts, anatomical errors (hands are a common problem), and unintended content.

**Do not assume generated images are factually accurate.** A generated image of "the interior of a Boeing 787" may look convincing but contain details that do not match the real aircraft. Use generated images for illustration, not documentation.

**Respect intellectual property.** Do not use image generation to knock off copyrighted designs, replicate another artist's distinctive style for commercial use, or generate images of real people without consent.

## Chapter Summary

Perplexity's visual capabilities work in two directions: understanding images you upload and generating new images from descriptions. Image analysis is broadly useful for identification, text extraction, and explanation. Image generation is powerful for content creation, concept visualization, and prototyping, though it has clear limits around consistency, text rendering, and technical precision. The most effective workflows combine visual and text features to move fluidly between research and visualization.

Up next: the Comet Browser, Perplexity's AI-native approach to web browsing.

# Chapter 15: The Comet Browser

## An AI-Native Approach to Web Browsing

For over three decades, web browsers have worked essentially the same way. You type a URL or search query, get a list of links, click through to websites, read, go back, click another link. The browser is a window into the web — but it does not help you understand what you are looking at.

Comet Browser changes that. Built by Perplexity, Comet is designed from the ground up to be AI-native. AI is not bolted on as an extension or sidebar — it is woven into the browsing experience. You can ask questions about the page you are reading, summarize articles, compare information across tabs, and get AI assistance without ever leaving the browser.

This chapter introduces Comet, explains what makes it different, walks through its key features, and covers Comet Plus — the subscription tier that supports publishers.

---

## What Makes Comet Different

Traditional browsers are passive. They fetch and display web pages, and that is about it. Everything else — understanding the content, extracting useful information, comparing sources, summarizing long articles — is left to you.

Comet is an active tool. It understands the content you are viewing and offers AI assistance in context. What that looks like in practice:

**On-page AI assistance.** While reading any web page, highlight text and ask Perplexity to explain it, summarize it, translate it, or research it further. The answer appears right there, in the browser, without switching to a separate tab or app.

**Intelligent summarization.** Land on a long article, research paper, or report? Comet summarizes it instantly, pulling out the key points so you can decide whether to invest time reading the full piece.

**Cross-tab awareness.** With multiple tabs open, Comet can draw connections between them. "Compare the pricing information on these two product pages" or "What do these three articles agree on, and where do they differ?" Something no traditional browser can do.

**Integrated search.** Comet's address bar doubles as a Perplexity search bar. Type a natural-language question and get a Perplexity answer directly, without navigating to perplexity.ai first.

**Contextual suggestions.** As you browse, Comet may offer relevant follow-up questions, related topics, or additional sources based on what you are reading. It anticipates your curiosity.

---

## Getting Started with Comet

Comet is available as a standalone application. To get started:

1. Download Comet from Perplexity's website.
2. Install it like any other browser.
3. Sign in with your Perplexity account to connect your search history, Spaces, and preferences.
4. Start browsing.

If you are coming from Chrome, Firefox, Safari, or Edge, the basic browsing experience will feel familiar. Tabs, bookmarks, an address bar, back and forward buttons — all the standard elements are there. The AI features layer on top of the conventional experience rather than replacing it.

You can import bookmarks, passwords, and browsing data from your previous browser to smooth the transition.

---

## Key Features in Detail

### Ask About Any Page

The feature you will use most often. While viewing any web page, activate Comet's AI panel (typically via a keyboard shortcut, a toolbar button, or by highlighting text). Then ask a question:

- "What is the main argument of this article?"
- "Summarize this page in three bullet points."
- "Is the data in this article consistent with recent studies on the same topic?"
- "Explain the technical terms on this page in plain language."
- "What are the credentials of this article's author?"

The AI reads the page content and responds in context. No copy-paste, no switching between applications. The workflow is seamless.

### Smart Summaries

Open a long page and Comet can generate an automatic summary. Particularly valuable for:

- **News articles.** Get the key facts in seconds without reading through filler paragraphs and ad breaks.
- **Research papers.** Understand the abstract, methodology, key findings, and conclusions without reading twenty pages.
- **Product reviews.** Extract the reviewer's verdict, pros, and cons from a lengthy review.
- **Legal and policy documents.** Understand the implications without parsing dense legal language.

### Text Selection Actions

Highlight any text on a page and Comet offers a menu of AI actions:

- **Explain** – get a plain-language explanation of the selected text.
- **Summarize** – condense the selected passage.

- **Translate** – convert the selected text to another language.
- **Research** – launch a Perplexity search on the selected topic.
- **Define** – look up the meaning of an unfamiliar term.

Faster than copying text, opening a new tab, navigating to a search engine or dictionary, and pasting it in. It keeps you in flow.

### Tab Comparison

Open two or more tabs with related content, then ask Comet to compare them. Useful for:

- **Shopping.** "Compare the specs and prices of the laptops on these two tabs."
- **Research.** "What do these three sources agree on about climate change projections?"
- **News.** "How does this outlet's coverage of the event differ from the coverage in my other tab?"

### Integrated Perplexity Search

The address bar accepts natural-language queries. Type a question instead of a URL and Comet delivers a Perplexity answer with citations – no need to navigate to the Perplexity website. You can also trigger a full Perplexity search, including Deep Research, right from the browser.

---

## Comet Plus

Comet is free to use. Comet Plus is an optional subscription at $5 per month that adds enhanced features and – importantly – supports the publishers whose content you browse.

### Why Comet Plus Matters

The web has a sustainability problem. Publishers create the content that search engines and AI systems draw on, but they increasingly struggle to monetize that content as users get answers without visiting their sites. Perplexity recognized the tension and, after abandoning its advertising model in February 2026, introduced Comet Plus to direct revenue to publishers.

When you subscribe to Comet Plus, a portion of your subscription fee is distributed to the publishers whose content you interact with through Comet. The more you read from a particular publisher, the larger their share. A direct financial link between content consumption and content creation — without ads, paywalls, or tracking.

### What Comet Plus Includes

Beyond supporting publishers, specific Comet Plus benefits continue to evolve — check Perplexity's pricing page for the current list. The core value proposition is clear: better browsing for you, and sustainable revenue for the publishers who make the open web worth browsing.

### The Bigger Picture

Comet Plus is an interesting experiment in internet economics. For years, the web has relied on advertising as its primary business model, with all the downsides that entails — tracking, privacy erosion, clickbait content, ad-blocker wars, and a user experience that often feels adversarial. Comet Plus offers an alternative: users pay a modest fee, publishers get compensated fairly, and the browsing experience remains clean and user-focused.

Whether the model succeeds at scale remains to be seen, but it is worth supporting if you believe in a web where quality content creation is economically viable.

---

## Comet vs. Browser Extensions

You might wonder whether you could get similar AI features by installing a Perplexity extension in your existing browser. Partially, but not fully.

Extensions can add AI sidebars and on-page tools to Chrome or other browsers, and Perplexity does offer such extensions. But they are limited by what the browser's extension system allows. They cannot deeply integrate with the rendering engine, the tab management system, or the address bar. They are guests in someone else's house.

Comet is purpose-built. The AI features are part of the browser's core architecture, which makes them faster, more tightly integrated, and capable of things an extension cannot do (like cross-tab awareness at the engine level).

Switching browsers is a significant commitment. If you are deeply embedded in Chrome's ecosystem (synced passwords, extensions, profiles, developer tools), the transition has a cost. Evaluate whether Comet's AI features add enough value to your daily workflow to justify the switch. For many people, the answer is yes. For some, a Perplexity extension in their existing browser may be sufficient.

---

## Privacy in Comet

Because Comet is AI-native, it processes more information about your browsing activity than a traditional browser. The AI needs to read page content to summarize, explain, and analyze it. That raises legitimate privacy questions.

Key points to consider:

- **What data is sent to Perplexity's servers?** When you use an AI feature on a page, the content (or relevant portions) is sent to Perplexity for processing. That is inherent to how the feature works.
- **When is data sent?** AI features are typically activated on demand — when you ask a question or request a summary. The browser is not constantly streaming everything you read to Perplexity's servers.
- **What about browsing history?** Review Comet's privacy settings to understand whether and how your browsing history is stored, synced, or used.
- **Sensitive browsing.** For pages containing sensitive personal, financial, or medical information, consider whether you want AI features active. You can typically disable AI features for specific pages or in private browsing mode.

We discuss privacy in depth in Chapter 24.

---

## Tips for Getting the Most Out of Comet

**Use keyboard shortcuts.** Learn the shortcut for activating the AI panel. The faster you can access it, the more naturally it becomes part of your flow.

**Be specific with questions.** "Tell me about this page" gives you a generic summary. "What evidence does this article present for its main claim?" gives you something useful.

**Use tab comparison for purchasing decisions.** Before buying anything significant, open the top contenders in separate tabs and ask Comet to compare them across the criteria that matter.

**Use smart summaries for triage.** When researching a topic, open several promising search results and use smart summaries on each to quickly identify which articles deserve full reading.

**Subscribe to Comet Plus if you read widely.** $5 per month to support the web publishers you rely on is a small price — and you get enhanced features in return.

---

## Perplexity Computer — Agentic AI Beyond Search

While Comet reimagines browsing, Perplexity Computer reimagines what an AI assistant can do on your behalf. Launched in February 2026 for Max subscribers and enterprise users, Perplexity Computer is agentic — it does not just answer questions, it takes actions.

Traditional Perplexity searches find information and present it. Perplexity Computer goes further: it performs multi-step tasks autonomously. Think of it as an AI agent that can navigate the web, interact with websites, fill out forms, gather data across multiple pages, and complete workflows that would otherwise require you to do each step manually.

### What Perplexity Computer Can Do

The system draws on 19 different AI models working in coordination to handle complex, multi-step tasks. Examples:

- **Web actions.** Book a restaurant reservation, find and compare flight options, or fill out an application form — tasks that require navigating and interacting with websites, not just reading them.
- **Multi-step research and execution.** "Find the three best-reviewed Italian restaurants near my hotel in Chicago, check availability for Saturday at 7 PM, and summarize the menus" — a task combining research, navigation, and synthesis.
- **Data gathering across sites.** Collect pricing from multiple vendor websites, compile product specifications from different manufacturers, or aggregate review scores from several sources into a single comparison.
- **Workflow automation.** Repetitive web-based tasks that follow a predictable pattern can be delegated, freeing you for work that requires human judgment.

### How It Differs from Deep Research

Deep Research reads and synthesizes information. Perplexity Computer reads, synthesizes, and acts. If Deep Research is a tireless research assistant, Perplexity Computer is a tireless executive assistant who can also carry out the tasks that research identifies.

### Availability and Access

Perplexity Computer is available to Max subscribers and enterprise users at $200/month. It is one of the fastest-evolving areas of the Perplexity platform — expect capabilities to expand significantly in the months following this book's publication.

---

## Chapter Summary

Comet reimagines web browsing with AI at its foundation. On-page questions, smart summaries, text selection actions, tab comparison, and integrated Perplexity search make it a more capable tool for anyone who spends significant time reading and researching online. Comet Plus adds enhanced features and, critically, directs revenue to the publishers who create the content you browse. Perplexity Computer extends the same agentic philosophy beyond the browser — autonomous, multi-step task execution for Max and enterprise users. Together they signal where Perplexity is heading: from answering questions to acting on your behalf.

Next chapter: Model Council — how to use multiple AI models simultaneously to get more reliable, nuanced answers.

# Chapter 16: Model Council

## Getting Multiple AI Perspectives on a Single Question

When you face an important decision, you do not ask one person for advice and stop there. You ask several people — each with different backgrounds, perspectives, and expertise — and synthesize their input. The same principle applies to AI.

Model Council is Perplexity's feature for doing exactly this. Instead of routing your query to a single language model, Model Council sends it to several models simultaneously and presents you with all their responses. You see how different AI systems interpret the same question, where they agree, where they diverge, and what each one brings.

This chapter explains how Model Council works, when it is most valuable, and how to use it well.

---

## Why Multiple Models Matter

Every large language model has its own training data, architecture, strengths, and blind spots. Different frontier models bring different strengths — Claude on nuanced reasoning, GPT on broad coverage, Gemini on multimodal tasks, Llama and Mistral on alternative training distributions. Model Council surfaces those differences side by side instead of forcing you to pick blind.

When you send a question to only one model, you get that model's perspective — including its biases, knowledge gaps, and stylistic tendencies. You have no way of knowing whether a different model would have given a substantially different (and potentially better) answer.

Model Council removes the blind spot. By showing you responses from multiple models side by side, it lets you:

- **Identify consensus.** When all models agree, your confidence in that answer can be higher.

- **Spot disagreements.** When models give conflicting answers, you know the topic is ambiguous, contested, or nuanced. Valuable information.
- **Choose the best response.** Sometimes one model nails the answer while others miss. You pick the best one.
- **Combine insights.** Each model might contribute something unique. The best answer might be a synthesis of elements from multiple responses.

---

## How to Use Model Council

Using Model Council is straightforward:

1. Enter your query in Perplexity as you normally would.
2. Select the **Model Council** option (this may appear as a toggle, a dropdown selection, or a dedicated mode depending on the interface).
3. Submit your query.
4. Perplexity sends your query to multiple AI models and displays the responses side by side or in sequence.
5. Review, compare, and use the responses as you see fit.

You do not need to select which models to include — Perplexity curates the council from its available roster. The specific models may vary and will likely evolve as new models are released and existing ones are updated.

---

## When to Use Model Council

Model Council is not something you need for every query. "What time zone is Tokyo in?" does not benefit from multiple perspectives. But for certain questions, Model Council pays off:

### Complex Analytical Questions

When you are asking a question that requires interpretation, judgment, or reasoning — not just fact retrieval — different models may approach it differently. "What are the most significant risks facing the electric vehicle industry over the next five years?" will get different emphasis and different risk factors from different models. The spread of responses gives you a more complete picture.

### Controversial or Debated Topics

Questions where reasonable people disagree are exactly where a single model's perspective can mislead. "Is remote work more productive than in-office work?" does not have a single correct answer. Model Council shows you how different models weigh the evidence and frame the tradeoffs.

### Creative Tasks

If you are writing, brainstorming, or looking for ideas, multiple models give you multiple starting points. "Write an opening paragraph for a blog post about sustainable fashion" yields different tones, angles, and hooks from different models. Pick the one that resonates or combine elements from several.

### Technical Questions with Multiple Approaches

Programming, architecture, and engineering questions often have multiple valid solutions. "What is the best way to implement authentication in a Node.js API?" might get you JWT-based solutions from one model, session-based from another, and OAuth-focused from a third. Seeing all approaches helps you make an informed choice.

### High-Stakes Research

When accuracy matters — medical questions (for informational purposes, not diagnosis), legal interpretations, financial analysis — cross-referencing multiple models reduces the risk of relying on a single model's error. If three models agree and one disagrees, you know where to focus your verification effort.

### When You Suspect Hallucination

If a response from a single model strikes you as possibly fabricated or inaccurate, running the same query through Model Council is a sanity check. If other models give a completely different answer, you know to investigate further.

---

## Reading Model Council Output

Multiple responses are only useful if you know how to read them. A practical approach:

### Step 1: Scan for Consensus

Read through all responses quickly, looking for points that appear in multiple answers. If three out of four models mention the same fact, framework, or recommendation, that is likely solid ground.

### Step 2: Note the Disagreements

Where do the models diverge? Here is where it gets interesting. Disagreement can mean:

- The question is genuinely ambiguous and the models are interpreting it differently.
- One model has more current or accurate information than the others.
- The models are drawing on different sources or weighting evidence differently.
- One or more models may be hallucinating.

### Step 3: Evaluate Quality

Not all responses are created equal. Look for:

- **Specificity.** Which response gives concrete details, examples, and data? Which stays vague?
- **Citations.** Which response points you to verifiable sources?
- **Reasoning.** Which response explains its logic rather than just stating a conclusion?
- **Caveats.** Which response acknowledges limitations, uncertainties, or alternative viewpoints? Often a sign of a higher-quality answer.

### Step 4: Synthesize

The best answer may not be any single model's response. It may be a combination — the structure from one, the data from another, the nuance from a third. Model Council gives you the raw material; synthesis is your job.

---

## Practical Examples

### Example 1: Investment Research

**Query:** "What are the pros and cons of investing in quantum computing stocks in 2026?"

Model A might focus on technical readiness and specific company positions. Model B might emphasize market size projections and timelines. Model C might highlight regulatory and geopolitical factors. Model D might take a cautious stance, noting the hype cycle. Together you get a more balanced view than any single model provides.

### Example 2: Content Strategy

**Query:** "What content formats are most effective for B2B SaaS marketing in 2026?"

One model might emphasize case studies and whitepapers. Another might push video and webinars. A third might highlight community-led content and thought leadership. The composite picture helps you build a more diversified content strategy.

### Example 3: Technical Architecture

**Query:** "What is the best database choice for a real-time analytics application handling 10 million events per day?"

Different models might recommend different databases — ClickHouse, Apache Druid, TimescaleDB, BigQuery Streaming — each with different trade-off analyses. Seeing all options with their pros and cons is more valuable than a single recommendation.

#### Example 4: Fact Checking

**Query:** "Did Denmark ban the sale of fossil fuel cars starting in 2030?"

If three models say yes with citations and one says no, you have a clear signal where consensus lies — and a prompt to verify with original sources. If models split evenly, the claim needs careful fact-checking.

---

## Model Council vs. Running Queries Sequentially

You could, in theory, achieve something similar by running the same query in Perplexity, then ChatGPT, then Claude, then Gemini. But Model Council has several advantages:

- **Speed.** All models respond simultaneously. You get every perspective in the time it takes one model to respond.
- **Consistency.** The exact same query is sent to all models. When you retype a query across platforms, you inevitably word it slightly differently, which affects the responses.
- **Convenience.** Everything is in one interface. No tab-switching, no copy-pasting, no managing multiple accounts.
- **Built-in comparison.** Responses are presented in a format designed for comparison, not scattered across different windows.

---

## Limitations

Model Council is powerful but has its limits:

- **More is not always better.** For straightforward factual queries, multiple responses just give you the same answer repeated four times. Use Model Council selectively.
- **It does not resolve disagreements for you.** When models disagree, Model Council shows you the disagreement but does not tell you which model is right. That judgment is yours.

- **You still need to verify.** If all four models confidently state the same incorrect fact, Model Council gives you false confidence. Cross-reference with primary sources for high-stakes decisions.
- **Resource consumption.** Model Council uses more computational resources than a single-model query. It may count as multiple queries against your usage limits.
- **Model availability.** The specific models available may change over time as Perplexity updates its offerings.

---

## Best Practices

**Use Model Council for important questions.** Do not waste it on trivia. Save it for decisions, analysis, creative work, and research where multiple perspectives add real value.

**Read all responses, not just the first one.** Tempting to read the first response and stop. Resist. The unique value of Model Council comes from comparison.

**Look for what is missing.** Sometimes the most valuable insight is not what the models say but what none of them mention. A conspicuous absence across all responses might indicate a blind spot in current AI knowledge.

**Use follow-up queries.** If Model Council reveals an interesting disagreement, ask follow-ups to explore it further. "Models A and C disagree about whether remote work reduces innovation. What does the empirical research say?"

**Combine with other Perplexity features.** Model Council works well as a starting point. Use the consensus to guide a Deep Research investigation, or take the best response and expand it into a Page.

---

## Chapter Summary

Model Council lets you query multiple AI models simultaneously, giving you a spread of perspectives on any question. Most valuable for complex analysis, controversial topics, creative tasks, technical decisions, and fact-checking. The key skill is reading the output effectively — identifying consensus, understanding disagreements, evaluating quality, and synthesizing the best elements from multiple responses. Use it for questions where multiple perspectives matter.

In the next chapter, we shift from features to technique, starting with the fundamentals of search and prompting in Perplexity.

# Part V: Search and Prompting Mastery

---

*"It is a capital mistake to theorize before one has data."*

— Arthur Conan Doyle

---

# Chapter 17: Search and Prompting Fundamentals

## Asking Questions That Get Great Answers

Perplexity is only as good as the questions you ask it. Not a criticism of the tool — it is the nature of any search or AI system. A vague question gets a vague answer. A precise, well-structured question gets a precise, useful answer.

The good news: asking great questions is a learnable skill. You do not need to memorize special syntax or learn a query language. You need to understand a handful of principles and develop the habit of applying them. This chapter teaches them.

---

## The Shift from Keywords to Natural Language

If you grew up with Google, you learned to search in keywords. Instead of typing a full question, you stripped it down to essential terms: "best laptop 2026 lightweight programming." That worked because traditional search engines matched keywords against web pages.

Perplexity works differently. It understands natural language. You can — and should — ask it full questions, the way you would ask a knowledgeable colleague:

- **Keyword style:** "best laptop lightweight programming 2026"
- **Natural language:** "What is the best lightweight laptop for a software developer in 2026, prioritizing battery life and keyboard quality?"

The natural-language version gives Perplexity far more to work with. It knows you are a developer (so it can prioritize relevant specs), that weight matters, that battery life and keyboard quality are your top criteria, and that you want current recommendations. The keyword version communicates almost none of that context.

Another pair to drive the point home:

- **Keyword style:** "protein powder side effects"
- **Natural language:** "I am a 40-year-old woman who just started strength training. Are there any side effects I should watch out for with whey protein powder, given that I have mild lactose intolerance?"

The second version tells Perplexity your age, sex, activity level, the specific supplement, and a relevant health condition. The answer you get back will be far more useful.

**The principle:** Write your queries as complete, specific questions. Include context, constraints, and criteria.

---

## The Five Elements of a Great Query

Most effective Perplexity queries contain some combination of five elements:

### 1. The Core Question

What do you want to know? State it clearly and directly.

- Weak: "Tell me about solar panels."
- Strong: "How much does a residential rooftop solar installation typically cost in the northeastern United States in 2026?"

### 2. Context

Give Perplexity the background it needs to tailor its response.

- "I am a small business owner with ten employees..."
- "I am a graduate student in molecular biology..."
- "I am planning a two-week trip to Japan in October..."

Context shapes the vocabulary, depth, and focus of the response. A question about tax deductions gets a different answer for a freelancer than a corporation.

### 3. Constraints

Define the boundaries of what you want.

- "Only consider options available in Canada."
- "Focus on studies published after 2022."
- "Limit the comparison to open-source tools."
- "Do not include options that cost more than $500."

Constraints prevent the response from going too broad.

#### 4. Criteria

When asking for recommendations, comparisons, or evaluations, tell Perplexity what matters to you.

- "Prioritize ease of use over advanced features."
- "I care most about reliability and customer support."
- "The most important factor is processing speed, followed by cost."

Without criteria, Perplexity has to guess what you value. It might guess wrong.

#### 5. Desired Format

Tell Perplexity how you want the answer structured.

- "Give me a bulleted list."
- "Present this as a comparison table."
- "Write a two-paragraph summary."
- "Organize your response with clear headings."

We go deeper into output formatting in Chapter 19, but even a simple format instruction sharply improves the usefulness of the response.

---

## Good Queries vs. Bad Queries: Side by Side

Seeing the difference between a mediocre query and a well-crafted one is the fastest way to internalize these principles. Study the pairs:

| Bad Query | Good Query | Why It Is Better |
|---|---|---|

| Bad Query | Good Query | Why It Is Better |
|---|---|---|
| "Tell me about AI." | "What are the three most significant applications of AI in healthcare diagnostics as of 2026?" | Narrows topic, specifies domain, limits scope, adds a time frame |
| "How do I invest?" | "What is a good strategy for a 35-year-old with $50,000 to invest in index funds through a Roth IRA?" | Adds age, amount, vehicle type, and account type |
| "Explain climate change." | "What are the main feedback loops that could accelerate climate change beyond current projections?" | Focuses on a specific mechanism rather than asking for a textbook chapter |
| "Best restaurants." | "What are the highest-rated Italian restaurants within walking distance of the Louvre in Paris, open on Mondays?" | Specifies cuisine, location, proximity constraint, and availability |
| "Is remote work good?" | "What does peer-reviewed research from the last three years say about the productivity effects of fully remote work in the software engineering industry?" | Specifies evidence type, time frame, work model, and industry |
| "Help with my resume." | "Review the following resume bullet point for a senior data analyst role and suggest a more impactful version that quantifies results: 'Managed data pipelines.'" | Gives the role, a specific task, a clear ask, and raw material to work with |

Every added detail narrows the response and lifts its relevance. You are not being demanding — you are being helpful. You are giving the AI what it needs to serve you well.

---

## Using Focus Modes Strategically

One of Perplexity's most powerful and most overlooked features is Focus modes. Choosing the right Focus mode before you type your query steers the sources Perplexity draws from, which directly affects the quality of the answer.

**Web** is the default and works well for general questions. If you are unsure which mode to use, Web is a safe choice.

**Academic** restricts sources to scholarly papers, journals, and research databases. Use it when you need peer-reviewed evidence, want to cite studies, or are exploring a technical topic in depth. For example: "What are the long-term cognitive effects of bilingual education in children under age 10?"

**Writing** shifts Perplexity into content-generation mode. It deprioritizes web search and focuses on producing original text. Use it when you want a draft, outline, or creative piece rather than a researched answer.

**Video** searches video content. Useful for tutorials, lectures, product reviews, and demonstrations. Try: "Find a video tutorial on setting up a home NAS server for beginners."

**Social** draws from community discussions on platforms like Reddit. Ideal for real-world opinions, user experiences, or troubleshooting advice. Example: "What do people actually think about the Pixel 9 after using it for six months?"

**Finance** pulls from SEC filings, corporate disclosures, earnings transcripts, and financial data. Use it for investment research, company analysis, or market questions. Example: "What were the key takeaways from Apple's most recent earnings call?"

**The rule of thumb:** If your question belongs to one of these categories, switch to that Focus mode before searching. Better sources, better answers.

---

## When to Use Pro Search

Standard search handles most queries well. But when your question is complex, multi-layered, or requires synthesizing information from many sources, Pro Search is worth the query credit.

Use Pro Search when:

- Your question has multiple parts that depend on each other.
- You need a comprehensive comparison across many dimensions.
- The topic is niche and reliable information is scattered across many sources.
- You want Perplexity to ask clarifying questions before diving in.

Do not waste Pro Search credits on simple factual lookups like "What time zone is Tokyo in?" or "Who directed The Godfather?" Standard search handles those instantly.

---

## Follow-Up Questions

A single query rarely gives you everything you need. Perplexity supports follow-ups within the same thread, and each one benefits from the context of the conversation so far.

Effective follow-up patterns:

**Drilling deeper.** "You mentioned federated learning. Can you explain how that works in more detail, with a concrete example?"

**Shifting focus.** "That was helpful. Now, what are the privacy concerns with the approach you described?"

**Challenging the response.** "You said remote work increases productivity, but I have read studies suggesting the opposite. What does the evidence show?"

**Requesting reformatting.** "Reorganize that information as a comparison table with columns for cost, difficulty, and time required."

**Narrowing scope.** "Great overview. Now focus specifically on how this applies to the financial services industry."

**Asking for sources.** "Point me to the primary studies behind the statistics you cited."

Follow-ups are one of Perplexity's biggest advantages over traditional search. In Google, every query starts from scratch. In Perplexity, each follow-up builds on what came before.

---

## Common Mistakes and How to Fix Them

### Being Too Broad

- **Mistake:** "Tell me everything about machine learning."
- **Fix:** "What are the three most common machine learning algorithms used in fraud detection, and how do they compare in accuracy?"

A request for "everything" is a textbook request, not a search query. Narrow to a specific aspect.

### Being Too Vague About What You Want

- **Mistake:** "Is this a good idea?"
- **Fix:** "I am considering switching from a salaried position to freelance consulting in UX design. What are the financial risks for someone with $15,000 in savings and no existing client base?"

Spell out what "this" is, what "good" means to you, and what context matters.

### Asking Multiple Unrelated Questions at Once

- **Mistake:** "What is the capital of Australia, and also how do I fix a leaking faucet, and what is the best CRM software?"
- **Fix:** Ask each question in its own thread.

Bundling unrelated questions produces disjointed answers. Group related questions; split unrelated ones.

### Assuming Perplexity Knows Your Situation

- **Mistake:** "Which programming language should I learn?"
- **Fix:** "I am a marketing professional with no coding experience. I want to automate data analysis tasks in spreadsheets and eventually build simple dashboards. Which programming language should I learn first?"

Perplexity does not know your budget, location, experience level, industry, or preferences unless you tell it.

### Not Choosing the Right Focus Mode

- **Mistake:** Searching for academic research on Web Focus and getting blog posts and news articles.
- **Fix:** Switch to Academic Focus before searching for research papers and peer-reviewed studies.

A few seconds spent selecting the right Focus mode saves you from sifting through irrelevant sources.

### Copying Someone Else's Prompt Verbatim

Prompts that work well in one context may not work in yours. A prompt designed for ChatGPT's creative writing mode is not ideal for Perplexity's research-focused approach. Understand the principles and craft your own queries.

---

## The Art of Iterative Research

The most effective Perplexity users do not expect a perfect answer on the first try. They iterate:

1. **Start broad.** Ask a general question to orient yourself. "What are the main approaches to carbon capture technology?"
2. **Identify what interests you.** The response mentions direct air capture, bioenergy with carbon capture, and ocean-based methods. Direct air capture sounds most relevant.
3. **Go deeper.** "What are the current costs and scalability challenges of direct air capture technology?"

4. **Get specific.** "Which companies are leading in direct air capture deployment, and what is their current operational capacity?"
5. **Challenge and verify.** "The cost figures you cited seem optimistic. What do skeptics say about the economics of direct air capture?"
6. **Synthesize.** "Based on everything we have discussed, summarize the current state and near-term outlook for direct air capture in a format I could present to my team."

The process mirrors how a skilled researcher works: start broad, narrow down, go deep, verify, and synthesize. Perplexity's thread-based conversation model is designed for exactly this workflow.

---

## When to Start a New Thread

Thread context is powerful, but it can also become a burden. If you have been asking about carbon capture for twenty messages and want to switch to something unrelated, start a new thread. The old context will only confuse things.

Start a new thread when:

- You are switching to a completely different topic.
- The current thread has become long and the AI seems to be losing track of earlier context.
- You want a fresh perspective unbiased by earlier responses in the thread.
- You are starting a new phase of research that does not depend on previous findings.

---

## Ready-to-Use Search Templates

These templates give you a head start for common research scenarios. Copy, customize, and use them directly.

### General Research

1. **Balanced overview:** "Give me a balanced overview of [topic], including the strongest arguments for and against, with citations to credible sources."

2. **Current state of the field:** "What is the current state of [field/technology] as of 2026? Include key players, recent breakthroughs, and unresolved challenges."

3. **Comparison:** "Compare [option A] and [option B] for [specific use case]. Present as a table with columns for [criterion 1], [criterion 2], [criterion 3], and overall recommendation."

### Professional and Business

4. **Competitive analysis:** "Who are the top five competitors to [company/product] in the [specific market] space? For each, list their main strengths, weaknesses, and pricing."

5. **Industry trend report:** "What are the three most important trends shaping the [industry] industry in 2026, and how should a mid-size company prepare for them?"

6. **Regulation check:** "What are the current regulatory requirements for [activity/product] in [jurisdiction]? Focus on changes from the last 12 months."

### Technical and How-To

7. **Step-by-step guide:** "Walk me through how to [specific task] step by step. I am a [experience level] and I am using [tool/platform/OS]."

8. **Troubleshooting:** "I am experiencing [specific problem] with [tool/system]. Here is what I have already tried: [list]. What else should I check?"

9. **Tool selection:** "I need a [type of tool] that supports [requirement 1] and [requirement 2]. My budget is [amount] and I need it for [use case]. What are the best options?"

### Academic and Learning

10. **Literature review starter:** "What are the most cited papers on [topic] published between [year] and [year]? Summarize the key findings from each." *(Use Academic Focus.)*

11. **Concept explainer:** "Explain [complex concept] in plain language, then give a technical explanation suitable for someone with a background in [field]."

12. **Study guide:** "I am studying for [exam/certification]. What are the most important topics to focus on, and what are common areas where people struggle?"

### Personal and Lifestyle

13. **Purchase decision:** "I am choosing between [product A] and [product B] for [specific use]. I care most about [criterion]. What do real users say after long-term use?" *(Use Social Focus.)*

14. **Travel planning:** "Plan a [number]-day itinerary for [destination] in [month]. I am interested in [interests], my budget is [amount] per day, and I prefer [travel style]."

15. **Health research:** "What does current medical research say about [health topic]? I am a [age/sex] with [relevant conditions]. Include citations to peer-reviewed sources." *(Use Academic Focus.)*

### Financial

16. **Company deep dive:** "Summarize [company]'s financial performance over the last four quarters. Include revenue trends, margins, and any guidance from the latest earnings call." *(Use Finance Focus.)*

17. **Market question:** "What are the main factors driving [market/sector] performance in 2026, and what are analysts forecasting for the next 12 months?" *(Use Finance Focus.)*

---

## Perplexity-Specific Tips

**Let Perplexity search.** Unlike ChatGPT or Claude, Perplexity's core strength is web search. Phrase queries in ways that benefit from real-time information: "What are the latest developments in..." or "What does recent research show about..."

**Check the sources.** Perplexity provides citations. Use them. Click through to the original sources for important claims. The citations are both a feature and a quality-control mechanism.

**Leverage suggested follow-ups.** Perplexity often suggests follow-up questions after a response. They are generated based on what is likely to be useful given your query. Worth reading even if you do not click — they may point you toward angles you had not considered.

**Use Pro Search for multi-step questions.** If your query involves comparing, evaluating, or synthesizing across multiple dimensions, Pro Search will often produce a substantially better answer than standard search.

**Match your Focus mode to your question.** Two seconds, real difference. Academic for research, Social for opinions, Finance for company data, Video for tutorials.

**Save recurring contexts in Spaces.** If you research the same topic repeatedly — a client project, a course you are taking — set up a Space with custom instructions so you do not re-explain the context every session.

---

## Chapter Summary

Great Perplexity results start with great questions. Use natural language, be specific, include context and constraints, specify your criteria, and request a format. Choose the right Focus mode and use Pro Search for complex queries. Follow up within threads to drill deeper, challenge responses, and refine your understanding. Avoid vague, overly broad, or context-free queries. Treat research as an iterative conversation, not a single query. Use the templates above as starting points and customize them for your needs. These fundamentals apply to every Perplexity feature and form the foundation for the advanced techniques in the next chapter.

# Chapter 18: Advanced Search Techniques

## Going Beyond Basic Queries

Chapter 17 gave you the fundamentals: be specific, provide context, iterate, and follow up. Those principles will carry you a long way. But to extract maximum value from Perplexity, there are advanced techniques experienced users rely on daily.

This chapter covers prompting strategies, source control, multi-step research workflows, and techniques for handling difficult or ambiguous questions.

---

## Prompt Engineering for Perplexity

The term "prompt engineering" gets thrown around a lot, and it sounds more complex than it is. At its core, it means structuring your input to get better output. Here are the techniques that matter most in Perplexity.

### Role Assignment

Tell Perplexity to adopt a specific role or perspective. This shapes the vocabulary, depth, and focus of the response.

- "As a patent attorney, analyze the patentability of the following invention concept..."
- "As a nutritionist, evaluate this meal plan for a 40-year-old with type 2 diabetes..."
- "As a senior software architect, review this system design and identify potential scalability bottlenecks..."

Role assignment works because it activates relevant knowledge patterns in the model. A response from the perspective of a patent attorney uses legal terminology, considers prior art, and focuses on novelty — things a generic response might miss.

### Chain-of-Thought Prompting

For complex analytical questions, ask Perplexity to show its reasoning step by step.

- "Walk me through the logic step by step: if the Federal Reserve raises interest rates by 0.5%, what are the likely cascading effects on the housing market, consumer spending, and tech sector valuations?"
- "Think through this systematically: what factors should I consider when choosing between a monolithic and microservices architecture for a startup's first product?"

This produces more thorough, more transparent answers. It also makes it easier to spot where the reasoning might be flawed.

### Constraint Stacking

Layer multiple constraints to narrow the response precisely to what you need.

"Find me peer-reviewed studies published after 2023, conducted in OECD countries, with sample sizes above 1,000 participants, that examine the relationship between remote work and employee mental health. Summarize the findings in a comparison table with columns for study, country, sample size, methodology, and key findings."

Each constraint (peer-reviewed, post-2023, OECD, sample size, topic) eliminates irrelevant results. The format instruction (comparison table) ensures usability.

### Negative Instructions

Sometimes the most effective way to shape a response is to tell Perplexity what not to do.

- "Do not include anecdotal evidence. Only cite empirical studies."
- "Do not recommend products from companies with fewer than five years of market presence."

- "Avoid technical jargon. Explain everything in terms a high school student would understand."
- "Do not give me a balanced view. I want the strongest arguments against this position."

Negative instructions are especially useful when you have seen Perplexity's default behavior and want to correct a specific tendency.

### The "Before You Respond" Technique

Ask Perplexity to do preliminary thinking before generating its answer.

"Before you respond, consider the following: I am asking this question because I need to make a decision about whether to invest in commercial real estate in Austin, Texas. I have a budget of $2 million. I am risk-averse and prioritize stable rental income over appreciation. With that context, what should I know about the Austin commercial real estate market in 2026?"

This front-loads the context and decision framework, producing a more targeted response.

---

## Source Control

Perplexity searches the web by default, but you have more control over sources than you might realize.

### Focus Modes

Perplexity offers Focus modes that constrain the source set:

- **Web** – the default. Searches the open web broadly.
- **Academic** – prioritizes scholarly sources, journals, and research databases.
- **Writing** – focuses on generating content rather than searching (useful for drafting tasks).
- **Video** – searches video content and can summarize videos.
- **Social** – searches Reddit, X, and forums for community discussions, opinions, and experiences.

- **Finance** – searches SEC filings, corporate disclosures, and financial data.

Choose the Focus mode that matches your query. An academic question about statistical methods benefits from Academic Focus. A question about real-world user experiences with a product benefits from Social Focus. A question about a company's financial performance benefits from Finance Focus. A how-to question might benefit from Video Focus if you learn better from video explanations.

### Explicit Source Instructions

Within your query, you can guide source selection:

- "Based on WHO and CDC data..."
- "According to the most recent IPCC report..."
- "Drawing on court filings and legal analysis, not news coverage..."
- "Using primary sources rather than secondary reporting..."

These do not guarantee specific sources, but they bias the search toward the types of sources you want.

### Evaluating Sources

Perplexity provides citations with every response. Develop the habit of evaluating them:

- **Is the source authoritative?** A peer-reviewed journal article carries more weight than a blog post.
- **Is it current?** A 2019 study may have been superseded by more recent research.
- **Is it relevant?** Sometimes a citation technically supports a claim but is about a different context or population.
- **Is it diverse?** If all citations come from a single source or a single perspective, the response may be presenting a one-sided view.

---

## Multi-Step Research Workflows

Advanced Perplexity users do not treat each query as isolated. They design workflows that build systematically toward comprehensive understanding.

### The Funnel Approach

Start broad and narrow progressively:

1. "What are the main categories of renewable energy storage technology?"
2. "Of those categories, which are most commercially viable for grid-scale deployment in 2026?"
3. "For the top two commercially viable options, what are the current costs per kilowatt-hour, and how have they trended over the past five years?"
4. "Which companies are leading in grid-scale deployment of [specific technology], and what is their installed capacity?"
5. "What are the main risks and challenges facing [specific company] in scaling their technology?"

Each step builds on the previous one, and the final output is far more useful than a single broad query could produce.

### The Debate Approach

Explore a topic from opposing perspectives:

1. "What is the strongest case for universal basic income?"
2. "What is the strongest case against universal basic income?"
3. "What do proponents say in response to the strongest criticisms?"
4. "What do opponents say in response to the strongest arguments in favor?"
5. "Where do both sides actually agree?"

This forces a thorough examination of an issue and protects against confirmation bias.

### The Triangulation Approach

Verify a claim by approaching it from multiple angles:

1. "What does academic research say about the effect of minimum wage increases on employment?"
2. "What do real-world case studies from cities and states that have raised their minimum wage show?"
3. "What do prominent economists on both sides of the debate argue?"
4. "What does the most recent meta-analysis on this topic conclude?"

If all four angles converge on a similar conclusion, you can be reasonably confident. If they diverge, you have identified real uncertainty.

### The Expert Simulation Approach

Use role assignment to get perspectives from different domain experts:

1. "As an environmental scientist, what are the main concerns about deep-sea mining?"
2. "As an economist, what are the economic arguments for and against deep-sea mining?"
3. "As an international law expert, what is the current legal framework governing deep-sea mining?"
4. "As a materials scientist, are there viable alternatives to deep-sea mining for obtaining these minerals?"

Each "expert" brings a different lens to the same issue, and the composite picture is richer than any single perspective.

---

## Handling Difficult Questions

Some questions are inherently hard for AI to answer well. Here are strategies for the trickiest categories.

### Questions with No Clear Answer

"What is the best programming language?" has no single correct answer. Instead of asking for "the best," ask for a framework:

"What factors should I consider when choosing a programming language for [specific use case], and how do the top three options compare against those factors?"

This transforms an unanswerable question into a useful analytical exercise.

### Questions About Very Recent Events

Perplexity searches the web in real time, so it handles current events better than static AI models. But very recent events (hours old) may not have comprehensive coverage yet. If you are asking about something that just happened:

- Specify that you want the most recent information available.
- Follow up after some time has passed for more comprehensive coverage.
- Cross-reference with multiple sources, as early reporting is often incomplete or inaccurate.

### Questions Requiring Quantitative Precision

"How many people in the United States have celiac disease?" sounds straightforward, but different sources cite different numbers depending on diagnostic criteria, survey methodology, and date. Ask for the range and the methodology:

"What is the estimated prevalence of celiac disease in the United States? Give me the range across major studies, including the methodology and date of each estimate."

### Questions That Trigger Safety Guardrails

AI models have safety filters that may prevent them from answering certain questions directly, even when the intent is legitimate (medical research, security analysis, historical atrocities). If you encounter a refusal:

- Reframe the question to make the legitimate purpose clear: "For an academic paper on cybersecurity vulnerabilities, explain how SQL injection attacks work and how to defend against them."
- Provide context about your role: "As a medical professional writing patient education materials, explain the risks of opioid use."

- Ask for the topic in a broader educational context rather than requesting specific instructions.

---

## Power User Patterns

### The Summary-First Pattern

"Give me a one-sentence summary, then a detailed breakdown with headings."

This gives you immediate understanding plus depth you can scan selectively.

### The Comparison Matrix Pattern

"Compare X, Y, and Z in a table with rows for: cost, ease of use, scalability, community support, and learning curve. Rate each as low, medium, or high."

Structured comparisons are one of the most useful outputs Perplexity can produce.

### The "What Am I Missing?" Pattern

After getting a response, ask: "What important aspects of this topic have we not covered yet?" or "What would an expert in this field say I should also consider?"

This surfaces blind spots in your own thinking and in the AI's initial response.

### The Source Audit Pattern

"For each claim in your response, rate your confidence level as high, medium, or low based on the quality and quantity of supporting sources."

This forces transparency about the strength of the evidence behind each point.

### The Counterargument Pattern

"Now argue the opposite position as strongly as you can."

After getting an answer that supports one side, this ensures you have considered the other.

---

## Combining Advanced Techniques with Perplexity Features

These prompting techniques become even more powerful when combined with Perplexity's features:

- **In Spaces:** Set advanced prompting patterns as custom instructions so every thread benefits from them automatically.
- **With Deep Research:** Use constraint stacking and the funnel approach to craft Deep Research queries that produce highly targeted outputs.
- **With Model Council:** Use the debate approach across multiple models to see how different AI systems handle the same analytical question.
- **With Pages:** Use the summary-first pattern and comparison matrix pattern to produce Pages that are immediately useful and well-structured.

---

## Chapter Summary

Advanced search in Perplexity is about strategy, not syntax. Role assignment, chain-of-thought prompting, constraint stacking, negative instructions, and multi-step workflows all sharply improve the quality of your results. Source control through Focus modes and explicit instructions ensures you are drawing on the right evidence. Multi-step workflows — funneling, debating, triangulating, and simulating expert perspectives — produce understanding that no single query can match. Master these techniques, and Perplexity becomes a real research partner rather than a fancy search engine.

# Chapter 19: Output Formatting and Control

## Getting Answers in the Shape You Need

A brilliant answer in the wrong format is only half useful. If you need a comparison table and get a wall of prose, you spend time reformatting. If you need a concise executive summary and get a ten-paragraph deep dive, you extract the key points yourself. The information is there, but it is not ready for use.

Perplexity gives you substantial control over how your answers are formatted. This chapter teaches you how to specify the structure, length, style, and presentation of responses so that what comes back is immediately usable — whether you are pasting it into a slide deck, forwarding it to a colleague, or feeding it into a spreadsheet.

---

## Why Formatting Matters

Formatting is not cosmetic. It is functional. The right format:

- **Saves time.** An answer that arrives in the format you need requires no post-processing.
- **Improves comprehension.** A bulleted list is easier to scan than a paragraph. A table makes comparison effortless. Headings create navigable structure.
- **Enables action.** A checklist invites completion. A decision matrix invites decision-making. A step-by-step guide invites execution.
- **Matches your output.** If your deliverable is a slide deck, you need bullet points. If it is a report, you need paragraphs with headings. If it is a database, you need structured data.

---

## Controlling Length

The simplest formatting instruction is length control. Here are effective ways to specify it:

### Word and Sentence Limits

- "Answer in one sentence."
- "Keep your response under 200 words."
- "Give me a two-paragraph answer."
- "Summarize in exactly five bullet points."

### Relative Length

- "Give me a brief overview." (Expect a few sentences to a paragraph.)
- "Provide a detailed analysis." (Expect several paragraphs with depth.)
- "Be thorough but concise." (Expect moderate length with high information density.)

### Level-Specific

- "Explain this at the level of a tweet." (~280 characters)
- "Give me an elevator pitch." (~30 seconds of reading)
- "Write enough to fill one page, single-spaced."
- "Provide an executive summary suitable for a one-page briefing."

When in doubt, be explicit about length. "Short" and "detailed" mean different things to different people. "Under 150 words" is unambiguous.

---

## Structural Formats

### Bulleted Lists

"List the top advantages of..." or "Give me the key points as bullets."

Bulleted lists work best for:

- Enumerating items without a specific order.

- Summarizing key takeaways.
- Presenting features, pros/cons, or options.
- Quick-scan reference material.

### Numbered Lists

"Walk me through the steps to..." or "Rank the following options from best to worst."

Numbered lists work best for:

- Sequential instructions (first do this, then do that).
- Rankings and prioritized lists.
- Procedures and processes.

### Tables

"Present this as a comparison table with columns for X, Y, and Z."

Tables are one of the most underused formatting requests, and they produce some of the most useful output. Use them for:

- Comparing products, services, or options across multiple criteria.
- Presenting data in rows and columns.
- Side-by-side analysis of two or more alternatives.
- Feature matrices.

Be specific about what goes in the rows and columns: "Create a table comparing Python, JavaScript, and Rust with rows for learning curve, performance, ecosystem size, and typical use cases."

### Headings and Sections

"Organize your response with clear headings and subheadings."

Essential for longer responses. Without headings, a 500-word response is a wall of text. With headings, it becomes a scannable document where you can jump to the section you need.

### Nested Structure

"Use main headings for each category and sub-bullets for specific items within each category."

Nesting is useful when you have hierarchical information — categories with items, topics with subtopics, departments with roles.

---

## Tone and Style Control

### Formality Level

- "Write in a formal, professional tone suitable for a board presentation."
- "Use a casual, conversational tone."
- "Write in plain English — no jargon, no acronyms."
- "Match the tone of a well-edited business magazine like Harvard Business Review."

### Audience Targeting

- "Explain this to someone with no technical background."
- "Write for a senior software engineer who is familiar with distributed systems."
- "This is for a group of high school students learning about economics for the first time."

Audience targeting is one of the most powerful formatting tools because it controls vocabulary, depth, example selection, and assumed knowledge all at once.

### Voice and Perspective

- "Write in the second person (you)."
- "Write in the third person for an objective report."
- "Write as a set of instructions using imperative mood (Do this. Check that. Verify the result.)."

---

## Specialized Output Formats

### Email Drafts

"Draft an email to my team announcing the new policy. Keep it professional but warm, under 200 words, with clear action items at the end."

Perplexity can draft emails, memos, and messages that you can copy, review, and send. Always review before sending — the model does not know your team's dynamics, inside jokes, or sensitivities.

### Code

"Write a Python function that takes a list of dictionaries and returns the top three entries sorted by the 'score' key."

For developers, Perplexity can produce code snippets, scripts, and longer programs. Specify the language, the purpose, and any constraints (libraries to use or avoid, style preferences, performance requirements).

### Markdown

"Format your response in Markdown with headers, bold for emphasis, and code blocks for any technical terms."

If you are pasting the output into a Markdown-compatible tool (GitHub, Notion, Obsidian, most CMS platforms), requesting Markdown formatting saves conversion time.

### JSON and Structured Data

"Return the information as a JSON object with keys for name, category, price, and rating."

Useful for developers and data analysts who need structured data they can programmatically process.

### Slide-Ready Content

"Format this as content for a five-slide presentation. Each slide should have a title, three to four bullet points, and a speaker note."

This does not create actual slides, but it gives you content you can drop into PowerPoint, Google Slides, or Keynote with minimal editing.

---

## Multi-Format Responses

You can request multiple formats in a single query:

"Give me a one-sentence summary, followed by a detailed analysis with headings, followed by a comparison table of the main options, followed by a bulleted list of recommended next steps."

Useful when your output serves multiple purposes — the quick summary for the email subject line, the detailed analysis for the report body, the table for the appendix, and the action items for the meeting agenda.

---

## Controlling What Is Included and Excluded

### Inclusion Instructions

- "Include specific numbers and statistics."
- "Include examples from real companies."
- "Include counterarguments to each point."
- "Include a section on limitations and caveats."
- "Include the source URL for each claim."

### Exclusion Instructions

- "Do not include background information — assume I already understand the basics."
- "Do not include disclaimers or caveats."
- "Skip the introduction and get straight to the analysis."
- "Do not repeat information from my previous question."
- "Exclude any options that require a paid subscription."

Exclusion instructions are underrated. They keep Perplexity from spending words on content you do not need, making the response more efficient and relevant.

---

## Reformatting Existing Responses

If Perplexity gives you a response in a format you do not like, you do not have to start over. Just ask for a reformat:

- "Convert that response into a bulleted list."
- "Reorganize that as a table."
- "Condense that into three sentences."
- "Expand the third point into a full paragraph."
- "Rewrite that for a non-technical audience."

Reformatting requests work on any previous response in the thread. Explore the content first, then shape the presentation.

---

## Templates for Common Formatting Needs

Here are ready-to-use templates for formatting requests you can adapt to your specific needs:

**For meeting prep:** "Summarize [topic] in a one-page format with sections for Background, Key Facts, Open Questions, and Recommended Discussion Points."

**For decision support:** "Present the options as a decision matrix with rows for each option and columns for cost, time to implement, risk level, and expected benefit. Include a recommendation at the bottom."

**For learning:** "Explain [topic] using the following structure: Simple Definition, Real-World Analogy, Detailed Explanation, Common Misconceptions, and Further Reading."

**For reporting:** "Write a brief report on [topic] with an Executive Summary (three sentences), Key Findings (bulleted list), Analysis (two to three paragraphs), and Recommendations (numbered list)."

**For social media:** "Write three versions of a social media post about [topic]: one for LinkedIn (professional), one for Twitter/X (concise and punchy), and one for a general audience newsletter."

---

## Best Practices

**Always specify format for complex queries.** The more complex the question, the more important the format instruction becomes.

**Front-load format instructions.** Put the format request at the beginning or end of your query, not buried in the middle where it might get lost.

**Combine format with length.** "Give me a bulleted list" plus "with no more than seven items" produces tighter, more useful output than an unconstrained list.

**Use format to force clarity.** A table forces the model to categorize information explicitly. A step-by-step list forces sequential clarity. The format itself becomes a thinking tool.

**Save your best formatting templates.** When you find a formatting pattern that works well for your recurring needs, save it somewhere you can reuse it. Better yet, set it as a custom instruction in a Space.

---

## Chapter Summary

Output formatting turns Perplexity from an answer engine into a production tool. By specifying length, structure, tone, audience, and format, you get responses that are immediately usable without post-processing. Tables, bulleted lists, headings, and specialized formats like email drafts and JSON let you match the output to your exact need. Reformatting existing responses lets you iterate on presentation without regenerating content. The formatting principles in this chapter apply to every other feature — Spaces, Pages, Deep Research, and regular search alike.

# Part VI: Perplexity for Your Field

*"All models are wrong, but some are useful."*

— George E. P. Box

# Chapter 20: Perplexity for Students and Educators

## AI-Powered Research in Academic Settings

If you are a student, Perplexity can sharply accelerate how you research, study, and learn. If you are an educator, it can transform how you prepare materials, design assignments, and support students. But both groups need to use it thoughtfully — because the same tool that helps you learn faster can also short-circuit learning entirely if misused.

This chapter addresses both audiences directly, with practical guidance on capturing the academic value of Perplexity while maintaining intellectual integrity.

---

## For Students

### Using Perplexity for Research

Perplexity is an outstanding research starting point. Notice the emphasis on "starting point." It excels at:

**Literature discovery.** "What are the most cited papers on the relationship between sleep and memory consolidation?" gives you a map of the research landscape. Use Academic Focus mode for best results.

**Concept explanation.** "Explain the difference between Type I and Type II errors in statistics, with examples" gives you a clear explanation to build on. When your textbook's explanation does not click, Perplexity can offer a different angle.

**Background research.** Before diving into a primary source, ask Perplexity for context: "Give me background on the Treaty of Westphalia and why it is significant in international relations." This helps you read the primary source with better comprehension.

**Source finding.** "What are the key primary sources for studying the American civil rights movement of the 1960s?" helps you build a bibliography. Always verify that the sources exist and say what Perplexity claims they say.

**Methodology understanding.** "Explain how a difference-in-differences research design works, and when is it appropriate to use one?" helps you understand the methods used in papers you are reading.

### What Perplexity Is Not

Perplexity is not a substitute for:

- **Reading primary sources.** Perplexity can summarize a paper, but summarizing is not understanding. Read the papers that matter to your work.
- **Original thinking.** Your thesis, your analysis, your argument — these must come from you. Perplexity can provide information and explain concepts, but the intellectual work of constructing an argument is yours.
- **A citation source.** Do not cite "Perplexity" as a source in academic papers. Cite the original sources that Perplexity points you to. Click through the citations, read the originals, and cite those.
- **A writing substitute.** Submitting AI-generated text as your own work is academic dishonesty at nearly every educational institution. Use Perplexity for research and understanding, not for generating the text you submit.

### Study Techniques with Perplexity

**Active recall testing.** Study a topic, then ask Perplexity to quiz you: "Ask me five questions about mitochondrial function that might appear on a cell biology exam." Answer them yourself before asking Perplexity to evaluate.

**Explanation practice.** The best way to test understanding is to explain something. Try explaining a concept in your own words, then ask Perplexity to identify what you got right, what you got wrong, and what you missed. "I think the Krebs cycle works like this: [your explanation]. What did I get right and what did I miss?"

**Analogies and alternative explanations.** When a concept is not clicking, ask for analogies: "Explain quantum entanglement using an everyday analogy."

Different explanations activate different mental models, and one of them might be the one that lands for you.

**Exam prep.** "What are the most commonly tested topics in an introductory macroeconomics course, and what are the key concepts I should be able to explain for each?" This helps you prioritize your study time.

**Writing feedback.** Paste a paragraph of your draft and ask: "What are the weaknesses in this argument? What counterarguments should I address? Is my reasoning sound?" Use the feedback to improve your own writing – do not ask Perplexity to rewrite it for you.

### Academic Integrity Guidelines

Every institution has its own policies on AI use, and those policies are evolving rapidly. Here is a practical framework:

1. **Know your institution's policy.** Check your university's academic integrity guidelines for specific rules about AI tool use. When in doubt, ask your professor.
2. **Disclose when required.** Some institutions require you to disclose AI tool usage. If so, be transparent about how you used Perplexity.
3. **Use it for research, not writing.** Use Perplexity to find sources, understand concepts, and explore topics. Write your papers yourself.
4. **Cite original sources.** Always trace Perplexity's citations back to the originals and cite those.
5. **Ask yourself the integrity test.** Would you be comfortable explaining exactly how you used Perplexity to your professor? If not, recalibrate your usage.

---

## For Educators

### Preparing Course Materials

Perplexity can sharply reduce preparation time:

**Lecture outlines.** "Create a lecture outline for a 50-minute class on the causes of World War I, suitable for first-year university history students. Include discussion questions." This gives you a solid draft to customize.

**Reading list curation.** "What are the ten most important papers on behavioral economics published in the last five years, and why is each significant?" This accelerates reading list development.

**Assignment design.** "Suggest five essay topics on the theme of social media and democracy, ranging from introductory to advanced difficulty. For each, suggest three sources students should consult." Use these as starting points and customize based on your course objectives.

**Exam question drafting.** "Generate ten multiple-choice questions on the cardiovascular system for a second-year anatomy course, with answer keys and brief explanations for each correct answer." Always review and adjust for accuracy and alignment with your teaching.

**Explanation alternatives.** When students struggle with a concept, use Perplexity to find alternative explanations and analogies: "What are three different ways to explain the concept of opportunity cost to students who are struggling with it?"

### Adapting to AI in the Classroom

AI tools are not going away, and pretending they do not exist is not a viable strategy. Here are approaches educators are using successfully:

**Teach AI literacy.** Dedicate class time to showing students how AI search tools work, what they are good at, and where they fail. Run a live demo where you ask Perplexity a question in your subject area and fact-check the response together. Students learn both the utility and the limitations.

**Design AI-resistant assignments.** Assignments that require personal reflection, connection to specific class discussions, analysis of datasets provided in class, or oral defense of written arguments are harder to outsource. This does not mean making assignments punitive — it means designing them so AI is a less useful shortcut.

**Design AI-integrated assignments.** Alternatively, some assignments can explicitly incorporate AI: "Use Perplexity to research [topic], then write a critical analysis of the AI's response, identifying what it got right, what it missed, and what it got wrong. Cite original sources to support your critique." This teaches both subject matter and AI literacy simultaneously.

**Use Perplexity as a classroom tool.** During lectures, pull up Perplexity live to demonstrate research techniques, fact-check claims in real time, or explore student questions on the fly. This models responsible AI use and shows students how to be critical consumers of AI output.

**Set clear policies.** Whatever your approach — prohibition, limited use, or full integration — communicate it clearly in your syllabus. Students need to know what is expected. "You may use AI tools for initial research and concept exploration. All submitted writing must be your own. Cite all sources, including any AI-generated content you used as a starting point."

### Detecting AI-Generated Work

This is a sensitive topic. AI detection tools exist, but they are unreliable — they produce both false positives (flagging human-written work as AI) and false negatives (missing AI-written work). A better approach:

- **Know your students' writing.** Early writing samples, in-class exercises, and drafts help you establish a baseline for each student's voice and ability.
- **Require process documentation.** Ask for outlines, drafts, annotations, and revision histories. AI can produce a final product instantly, but it cannot easily produce a believable process trail.
- **Oral examination.** If you suspect a submission was AI-generated, ask the student to explain their work verbally. Someone who wrote and understood their paper can discuss it fluently.
- **Focus on learning over policing.** The goal is education, not catching cheaters. Design your teaching so that using AI as a shortcut disadvantages the student's learning, and most students will choose to do the real work.

---

## Perplexity for Specific Academic Contexts

### STEM Students

Use Academic Focus mode for finding peer-reviewed research. Ask Perplexity to explain complex equations, experimental methodologies, and technical concepts. Upload lab reports or data sets for analysis assistance. But always verify quantitative claims — AI systems make mathematical errors.

### Humanities Students

Use Perplexity for historical context, biographical information, and finding primary source collections. Ask it to explain philosophical arguments, literary theories, or historical debates. But remember that interpretation and argumentation are the core skills of the humanities — these must come from you.

### Graduate Students

Perplexity is especially valuable for literature reviews, methodology exploration, and interdisciplinary research where you need to understand concepts from outside your field. Use Deep Research for comprehensive literature surveys. Create Spaces for each major research project with custom instructions tailored to your field.

### Language Learners

Use Perplexity in your target language. Ask questions in that language and read the responses as a form of immersion. Ask for translations, grammar explanations, and cultural context. Upload texts in the target language and ask for analysis.

---

## A Note on Evolving Norms

The role of AI tools in education is evolving rapidly. Policies that exist today will change. New tools will emerge. The core principles, however, are stable: use AI to enhance your learning, not to replace it. Be transparent about your usage. Develop your own critical thinking, not just your ability to prompt an AI. These will serve you well regardless of how the specific tools and policies evolve.

## Chapter Summary

For students, Perplexity is a powerful research accelerator and study aid — but it is not a substitute for reading, thinking, or writing. Use it to discover sources, understand concepts, test your knowledge, and get feedback on your reasoning. For educators, Perplexity can streamline course preparation and offer new pedagogical approaches that teach both subject matter and AI literacy. Both groups benefit from clear expectations, transparent usage, and a focus on genuine learning.

# Chapter 21: Perplexity for Business and Teams

## Turning AI Search into a Competitive Advantage

Every business runs on information. Market intelligence, competitive analysis, customer research, regulatory updates, technical documentation, financial data – the companies that find, process, and act on information faster than their competitors win. Perplexity, used strategically, is a serious force multiplier for that information advantage.

This chapter covers how individuals, teams, and organizations can integrate Perplexity into their business workflows, from solo entrepreneurs to enterprise teams.

---

## Individual Business Use Cases

### Market Research

Before launching a product, entering a market, or making a strategic decision, you need to understand the landscape. Perplexity accelerates this sharply:

- "What is the current market size for plant-based protein in Southeast Asia, and what is the projected growth rate through 2030?"
- "Who are the top five competitors in the fleet management software space, and what differentiates them?"
- "What regulatory changes are expected in the EU fintech sector in 2026–2027?"

Use Deep Research for comprehensive market analyses. Use standard search for quick fact-checking and data points. Use Model Council for questions where you want multiple analytical perspectives.

### Competitive Intelligence

Stay informed about what your competitors are doing:

- "What has [Competitor Name] announced in the last 90 days regarding new products, partnerships, or leadership changes?"
- "Compare [Competitor A]'s pricing model with [Competitor B]'s. What are the implications for a mid-market customer?"
- "What are customers saying about [Competitor Name] on Reddit and review sites?"

Create a Space for competitive intelligence with custom instructions to focus on your industry, your competitors, and the metrics that matter to you. Every thread in that Space applies those filters automatically.

### Sales and Business Development

- "Summarize [Company Name]'s recent earnings call, focusing on their priorities for the next fiscal year."
- "What pain points do IT directors at mid-market healthcare companies typically face with their current data infrastructure?"
- "Research the attendee list for [Conference Name] and identify the companies most likely to be interested in our product."

This kind of research used to take hours of manual digging. Perplexity compresses it to minutes.

### Content and Marketing

- "What topics are trending in the B2B SaaS marketing space this month?"
- "Analyze the top-performing blog posts on [Competitor's blog URL] and identify common themes."
- "Draft five LinkedIn post ideas for a cybersecurity company targeting healthcare CIOs."

Use Perplexity for research and ideation. Use your own voice and expertise for the final content.

### Financial Analysis

- "Summarize the key financial metrics from [Company Name]'s most recent 10-K filing."
- "What are analysts saying about the outlook for the semiconductor industry in H2 2026?"
- "Compare the PE ratios of the top five cloud infrastructure companies and explain what the differences suggest."

Always verify financial data against primary sources (SEC filings, earnings reports, analyst reports from reputable firms). Perplexity excels at finding and summarizing this data, but financial decisions demand verified numbers.

---

## Team Workflows

### Shared Spaces for Team Research

Spaces are the backbone of team-based Perplexity use. Here is how to structure them:

**One Space per project or initiative.** "Q3 Product Launch," "European Expansion Research," "2026 Budget Planning." Each Space gets its own custom instructions, uploaded reference materials, and collaborators.

**Standardize custom instructions.** Define how the AI should respond for your team's context: industry terminology, preferred sources, formatting standards, and depth level. This keeps research consistent across team members.

**Upload shared reference materials.** Company style guides, product documentation, internal research reports, competitor profiles — upload them to the Space so every team member's queries can draw on the same reference base.

**Assign roles thoughtfully.** Give admin access only to people who should be modifying custom instructions. Give contributor access to active researchers. Use viewer access for stakeholders who need to see the research but should not alter the setup.

### Collaborative Research Patterns

**Divide and conquer.** In a team Space, assign different sub-topics to different people. One person researches pricing trends, another technology trends, a third regulatory changes. All threads live in the same Space, building a comprehensive knowledge base.

**Review and build.** One team member starts a thread with initial research. Others review it and start follow-up threads that go deeper on specific aspects. The Space becomes a layered investigation.

**Create Pages from team research.** After the research phase, consolidate findings into Pages that can be shared with stakeholders outside the team. Pages serve as the polished output of the team's collective work.

---

## Enterprise Features

### Enterprise File Sync

For larger organizations, Perplexity's enterprise tier offers file sync with cloud storage platforms. This means your Spaces can automatically stay current with documents stored in Google Drive, SharePoint, Dropbox, or similar services.

The practical impact: when someone in your organization updates a pricing document, a policy manual, or a research report in the shared drive, the connected Space picks up the changes automatically. No one has to remember to re-upload files. The model always has the latest versions.

### Data Protection

Enterprise plans typically include stronger data protection guarantees:

- **No training on your data.** Your uploaded files and queries are not used to improve Perplexity's models.
- **Data isolation.** Your organization's data is kept separate from other customers' data.
- **Compliance features.** Support for regulatory requirements like GDPR, SOC 2, and industry-specific compliance standards.

- **Admin controls.** Organization-wide settings for data retention, user management, and access controls.

If your organization handles sensitive data — and most do — the enterprise tier's data protection features are not optional. They are a baseline requirement.

### Team Analytics

Enterprise plans may include usage analytics that help administrators understand how the team is using Perplexity: which features are used most, which Spaces are most active, and where the tool delivers the most value. This data helps justify the investment and identify opportunities for broader adoption.

---

## Department-Specific Applications

### Product Management

- Research competitive features and market positioning.
- Upload product requirements documents and ask Perplexity to identify gaps or inconsistencies.
- Generate comparison matrices for build-vs-buy decisions.
- Use Deep Research for comprehensive market analysis reports.

### Human Resources

- Research compensation benchmarks for specific roles and geographies.
- Stay current on employment law changes.
- Draft job descriptions based on industry standards.
- Research best practices for employee engagement and retention.

### Legal

- Research case law and regulatory precedents (always verify with primary legal sources).
- Summarize long legal documents and contracts.
- Stay current on regulatory changes in relevant jurisdictions.
- Upload contracts for clause comparison and risk identification.

### Customer Success

- Research a customer's industry and recent news before a quarterly business review.
- Upload support tickets or feedback data and ask for pattern analysis.
- Research best practices for reducing churn in your market segment.

### Operations

- Research supply chain alternatives and logistics options.
- Upload process documentation and ask for efficiency improvement suggestions.
- Stay current on industry standards and certification requirements.

---

## Return on Investment

Perplexity is not free for business use (the features that matter most require Pro, Max, or Enterprise plans), so it is worth thinking about return on investment.

The primary value is time savings. Consider:

- A market research task that takes a business analyst four hours manually might take thirty minutes with Perplexity.
- Competitive intelligence that requires monitoring dozens of sources daily can be streamlined into a few focused Perplexity queries.
- Meeting preparation that involves reading multiple reports can be compressed into uploaded summaries.

If a Pro subscription saves a knowledge worker two hours per week — a conservative estimate for active users — the subscription pays for itself many times over in productivity gains.

The secondary value is quality. Perplexity's ability to search broadly, cite sources, and cross-reference means the research output is often more comprehensive than what a time-pressed employee would produce manually. You get both speed and breadth.

---

## Implementation Best Practices

If you are rolling out Perplexity across a team or organization:

**Start with a pilot.** Identify a team or project where Perplexity can add clear value. Run a focused pilot, measure the results, and use that data to justify broader adoption.

**Train your team.** The techniques in Chapters 17–19 (search fundamentals, advanced search, output formatting) make a serious difference in results quality. Invest time in teaching your team how to prompt effectively.

**Establish guidelines.** Create clear policies on what can and cannot be uploaded to Perplexity, how research should be attributed, and what types of decisions should be double-checked against primary sources.

**Create shared Spaces for recurring needs.** Do not let every team member reinvent the wheel. Build well-configured Spaces for common research needs — competitive intelligence, market research, product comparison — with tested custom instructions and uploaded reference materials.

**Measure impact.** Track time savings, research quality improvements, and user satisfaction. These metrics justify the investment and guide optimization.

---

## Limitations for Business Use

- **Not a replacement for domain expertise.** Perplexity accelerates research, but it cannot replace the judgment of experienced professionals.
- **Verify before acting.** For high-stakes decisions — financial, legal, medical, regulatory — always verify AI-generated research against primary sources.
- **Confidentiality.** Be mindful of what you type into queries. On non-enterprise plans, your queries may be stored or used in aggregate. Do not include proprietary information, trade secrets, or personal data in queries unless you are on an enterprise plan with appropriate data protections.
- **Not a database.** Perplexity is a research and analysis tool, not a data warehouse. Do not try to use it as your system of record.

## Chapter Summary

Perplexity is a natural fit for business use across nearly every function — from market research and competitive intelligence to content creation and financial analysis. Team features like Spaces with shared files, custom instructions, and collaboration make it possible to standardize and scale AI-powered research across an organization. Enterprise features add the data protection, compliance, and administration capabilities serious organizations require. The key to business value is strategic adoption: clear use cases, trained users, shared resources, and thoughtful policies.

# Chapter 22: Perplexity for Developers

## Building with the Sonar API and Beyond

Perplexity is not just a consumer product. It is also a developer platform. Through the Sonar API, you can integrate Perplexity's search-augmented AI capabilities into your own applications, workflows, and products. This chapter covers both using Perplexity as a developer tool day to day and building with the API.

---

## Using Perplexity in Your Development Workflow

Before the API, here is how Perplexity helps you as a developer day to day.

### Researching Technologies

The technology landscape moves fast. Perplexity helps you stay current:

- "What are the key differences between Next.js and React Router for server-side rendering in 2026?"
- "Compare the performance characteristics of PostgreSQL, CockroachDB, and Supabase for a multi-region application."
- "What are the current best practices for containerized CI/CD pipelines using GitHub Actions?"

Use Academic Focus for research papers on algorithms and systems. Use standard Web Focus for practical guides, documentation, and community discussions.

### Debugging and Problem Solving

When you hit an error or an unexpected behavior:

- "Explain this error message: [paste the error]. I am running Python 3.13 on Ubuntu 24.04 with FastAPI."

- “Why might a React component re-render excessively even when its props have not changed?”
- “What are the common causes of memory leaks in a Go application using goroutines?”

Providing full context — language version, framework, operating system, and the exact error — sharply improves the quality of the response.

### Architecture and Design Decisions

- “What are the tradeoffs between event sourcing and traditional CRUD for an e-commerce order management system?”
- “When should I use a message queue versus direct API calls for microservice communication?”
- “What are the security implications of using JWTs versus session cookies for authentication in a public-facing API?”

Use Model Council for architecture questions where you want multiple perspectives, or Deep Research for thorough evaluations of complex design decisions.

### Code Review and Understanding

Upload code files or paste code snippets and ask for analysis:

- “Review this Python function for potential bugs, performance issues, and readability improvements.”
- “Explain what this SQL query does step by step.”
- “What are the security vulnerabilities in this Node.js authentication middleware?”

### Documentation Research

- “Summarize the breaking changes in the Django 5.2 release notes.”
- “What is the correct syntax for creating a composite index in MongoDB?”
- “How do I configure CORS in a Rust Actix-web application?”

Perplexity searches documentation sites, Stack Overflow, GitHub issues, and blog posts — often faster than navigating documentation yourself.

## The Sonar API

The Sonar API is Perplexity's developer interface. It lets you programmatically access Perplexity's search-augmented AI capabilities and embed them in your own applications.

### API Overview

The Sonar API provides access to a family of models, each optimized for different use cases:

| Model | Description | Best For |
|---|---|---|
| **sonar** | Fast, efficient search-augmented responses | Quick factual queries, high-volume applications |
| **sonar-pro** | Higher quality, more thorough responses | Complex questions, detailed analysis |
| **sonar-reasoning-pro** | Most capable reasoning model | Complex analytical tasks requiring deep reasoning |
| **sonar-deep-research** | Multi-step research investigations | Comprehensive research, detailed reports |

### Getting Started

To use the Sonar API:

1. **Create a Perplexity account** and navigate to the API settings or developer portal.
2. **Generate an API key.** This key authenticates your requests.
3. **Choose your model.** Select the Sonar model that matches your use case.
4. **Make API calls.** The API follows standard conventions. You send a POST request with your query and receive a JSON response.

### Basic API Call

The Sonar API uses a chat completions format similar to other LLM APIs. A basic request looks like this:

```
POST https://api.perplexity.ai/chat/completions

{
  "model": "sonar",
  "messages": [
    {
      "role": "system",
      "content": "You are a helpful research assistant."
    },
    {
      "role": "user",
      "content": "What are the latest developments in solid-state battery techno
logy?"
    }
  ]
}
```

The response includes the AI-generated answer along with citations — the URLs of the sources that informed it. This is the key differentiator of the Sonar API: every response comes with source attribution.

### Citations in API Responses

Unlike generic LLM APIs, Sonar API responses include a `citations` array listing the URLs of sources used. This means you can:

- Display source links alongside AI-generated content in your application.
- Allow users to verify claims by clicking through to original sources.
- Build trust by showing where the information comes from.
- Create transparency features that set your application apart from competitors using opaque AI.

### Choosing the Right Model

**sonar** — Use when you need fast, affordable responses for straightforward factual queries. Ideal for chatbots, FAQ systems, and high-volume applications where speed and cost matter more than depth.

**sonar-pro** — Use when you need more detailed, nuanced responses. Ideal for research tools, content generation, and applications where quality justifies higher cost and latency.

**sonar-reasoning-pro** — Use when your application needs to solve problems, not just retrieve information. Ideal for analytical tools, decision-support systems, complex technical questions, and applications where reasoning quality is paramount.

**sonar-deep-research** — Use for comprehensive, multi-step investigations. Ideal for research platforms, due diligence tools, and applications that produce detailed reports. Deep research requests take much longer to complete.

### API Use Cases

**Search-augmented chatbots.** Build a customer-facing chatbot that can answer questions with current, cited information rather than relying on a static knowledge base.

**Research automation.** Create workflows that automatically research topics, compile findings, and generate reports on a schedule.

**Content enrichment.** Enhance your content management system by automatically adding context, related information, and citations to articles.

**Monitoring and alerts.** Build systems that periodically query the API for updates on specific topics and alert you when new information is available.

**Data enrichment.** Augment your database records with current information from the web. For example, automatically update company profiles with recent news and financial data.

**Internal tools.** Build company-specific research tools that combine the Sonar API with your internal data to give employees a unified research interface.

---

## Building Applications with Sonar

### Architecture Considerations

When integrating the Sonar API into your application:

**Handle latency appropriately.** API calls to Sonar models take longer than calls to non-search-augmented LLMs because they include a web search step.

Design your UI to handle this — loading indicators, streaming responses, or asynchronous processing.

**Implement caching.** For queries likely to be repeated (common questions, FAQ-type queries), cache the responses. This reduces API costs and improves response times. Be thoughtful about cache expiration — the web changes, and cached responses go stale.

**Manage rate limits.** Check the API documentation for rate limits associated with your plan. Implement retry logic with exponential backoff for rate-limited requests.

**Handle errors gracefully.** Network failures, rate limits, and occasional API errors are facts of life. Handle them without crashing or confusing the user.

**Respect the citations.** If you display Sonar API responses to users, display the citations too. This is both ethically important (giving credit to sources) and practically valuable (building user trust).

### Streaming Responses

The Sonar API supports streaming, which lets you display the response as it is generated rather than waiting for completion. This sharply improves perceived performance. Implement streaming if your application has a user-facing chat or response interface.

### System Prompts

Use the system message to customize the AI's behavior for your application:

```
{
  "role": "system",
  "content": "You are a medical information assistant for a healthcare app.
  Always include a disclaimer that your responses are for informational
  purposes only and do not constitute medical advice. Cite peer-reviewed
  medical sources when possible. Respond in clear, non-technical language."
}
```

System prompts let you customize tone, focus, constraints, and formatting without the user needing to specify these in every query.

## API Pricing and Optimization

The Sonar API is priced based on usage (tokens processed). To manage costs:

- **Choose the right model.** Do not use sonar-reasoning-pro for simple factual queries that sonar handles fine.
- **Optimize prompts.** Concise, well-structured prompts consume fewer input tokens.
- **Cache intelligently.** Cache responses for repeated queries with appropriate expiration.
- **Set token limits.** Use the `max_tokens` parameter to cap response length when you know a short answer suffices.
- **Monitor usage.** Track your API consumption to identify unexpected spikes and optimize accordingly.

---

## Integrating with Other Tools

The Sonar API works well alongside other development tools and APIs:

- **LangChain and similar frameworks.** Sonar can be integrated as a tool or retrieval mechanism within LLM orchestration frameworks.
- **Webhooks and automation platforms.** Connect Sonar API calls to Zapier, Make, or custom webhook handlers for automated research workflows.
- **Database systems.** Use Sonar to enrich database records, then store the enriched data for querying.
- **CI/CD pipelines.** Build automated documentation updates, dependency research, or changelog generation into your development pipeline.

---

## Best Practices for Developers

**Read the API documentation.** This chapter provides an overview, but the official docs have the latest endpoints, parameters, rate limits, and model details. Start there for implementation.

**Start with sonar.** Begin with the fastest, most affordable model. Only upgrade to sonar-pro or sonar-reasoning-pro when you have a demonstrated need for additional quality.

**Test with realistic queries.** Your test queries should resemble what your users will ask. Synthetic test queries often produce misleadingly good results.

**Monitor response quality.** Set up logging to review a sample of API responses regularly. Quality can vary, and catching issues early prevents user-facing problems.

**Plan for model updates.** Sonar models evolve. New versions may produce different outputs. Test your application against new model versions before deploying them to production.

---

## Chapter Summary

For developers, Perplexity serves two roles: a daily tool for research, debugging, and architectural decisions, and a platform for building search-augmented AI applications via the Sonar API. The Sonar family spans five models from fast and efficient (sonar) to comprehensive (sonar-deep-research), each with built-in web search and citation support. When building with the API, focus on choosing the right model, handling latency gracefully, respecting citations, and optimizing for cost. Real-time search plus AI reasoning makes the Sonar API a distinctive building block for applications that need current, sourced information.

# Part VII: Limitations, Safety, and Ethics

---

*"Trust, but verify."*

— Russian proverb

---

# Chapter 23: What Perplexity Gets Wrong

## An Honest Look at Limitations and Failure Modes

Every tool has limits. A saw cannot drill holes. A spreadsheet cannot write poetry. And Perplexity — for all its capabilities — has specific, identifiable failure modes you need to understand. Not because the tool is bad, but because knowing where it breaks is the difference between using it wisely and being misled by it.

This chapter catalogs the ways Perplexity can fail, explains why those failures happen, and gives you practical strategies for catching and mitigating them.

---

## Hallucination

This is the big one. Hallucination is when the AI generates information that sounds plausible but is factually incorrect. It might cite a study that does not exist, attribute a quote to someone who never said it, invent a statistic, or describe a historical event that never happened.

### Why It Happens

Large language models generate text by predicting the most likely next token (word or word fragment) based on patterns in their training data. When the model lacks reliable information on a topic, it does not say "I don't know." It generates the most plausible-sounding response it can construct. Sometimes that response is wrong.

Perplexity's search-augmented approach reduces hallucination sharply compared to standalone LLMs, because it grounds responses in real web sources. But it does not eliminate the problem. The model may misinterpret a source, combine information from multiple sources incorrectly, or fill in gaps between sources with plausible-sounding but unsupported claims.

### How to Catch It

- **Check the citations.** Click through to the cited sources and verify they say what the response claims.
- **Cross-reference.** Run the same query again, or use Model Council to see if multiple models agree.
- **Be skeptical of specifics.** Hallucinated statistics, dates, and names are especially common. If a specific data point matters to your decision, verify it independently.
- **Watch for unusual confidence.** If the response is highly confident about something surprising or counterintuitive, that is a signal to verify.

---

## Source Quality Issues

Perplexity searches the web and cites what it finds. But the web is not uniformly reliable. Sometimes Perplexity cites:

- **Outdated information.** An article from 2019 presented as current in a 2026 context.
- **Low-authority sources.** Blog posts, opinion pieces, or marketing content presented alongside — or instead of — authoritative sources.
- **Misleading sources.** Content that technically contains the keywords Perplexity searched for but does not support the claim it is cited for.
- **Paywalled abstracts.** Perplexity may cite a paper based on its abstract alone, missing nuances in the full text.

### How to Mitigate

- **Use Academic Focus mode** for research questions requiring reliable sources.
- **Specify source constraints** in your query: "Cite only peer-reviewed sources" or "Prioritize government statistics."
- **Evaluate the source list.** Scroll through the citations and note the types of sources. If they are all blogs and forums, the response may not be reliable enough for your needs.

- **Follow up.** "Are there any primary sources (government data, peer-reviewed studies) that confirm these claims?"

---

## Recency Gaps

Perplexity searches the web in real time, which is a major advantage. But "real time" does not mean "instantaneous":

- Very recent events (hours old) may not yet be covered by indexed web sources.
- Some topics update faster than the available web content. Financial data, for example, may be quoted from a source that is hours or days old.
- Sources that update slowly (government statistics, annual reports) may lag the reality by months.

### How to Mitigate

- **Ask about the date of the data.** "When was this data last updated?"
- **Specify recency requirements.** "Only cite sources from the past six months."
- **Cross-reference with real-time sources.** For financial data, check live market feeds. For news, check major news outlets directly.

---

## Reasoning Errors

Perplexity can struggle with certain types of reasoning:

### Mathematical Errors

AI language models are not calculators. They make arithmetic mistakes, misapply formulas, and produce incorrect quantitative results. This is especially true for multi-step calculations, unit conversions, and statistical analysis.

If your query involves math, verify the calculations independently. Do not trust AI-generated numbers without checking them.

### Logical Fallacies

The model may construct arguments that contain logical fallacies — false equivalences, circular reasoning, cherry-picked evidence, or correlation-causation confusion. These are often subtle and demand critical reading to catch.

### Overconfident Conclusions

The AI may present a conclusion with more certainty than the evidence warrants. A handful of studies with mixed results might be summarized as "research shows" without acknowledging the uncertainty. Look for hedging language — or the conspicuous absence of it.

---

## Context Window Limitations

In long threads with many messages, the AI's ability to recall and use information from earlier in the conversation degrades. This is an architectural limitation of language model context windows.

### Symptoms

- The AI contradicts something it said earlier in the thread.
- It asks for information you already provided.
- It loses track of constraints or preferences you specified earlier.
- The quality of responses degrades as the thread grows longer.

### How to Mitigate

- **Start new threads** for new topics or when threads get long.
- **Repeat key context** in important follow-up queries: "Remember, I am focused specifically on the Canadian market."
- **Use Spaces with custom instructions** for persistent context that should apply to every message.

---

## Bias

The AI reflects the biases present in its training data and in the web sources it cites. These biases can manifest as:

- **Cultural bias.** Defaulting to a US-centric perspective on global topics.
- **Temporal bias.** Overweighting recent trends and underweighting historical context.
- **Source bias.** Citing English-language sources disproportionately, even when excellent sources exist in other languages.
- **Popularity bias.** Featuring widely covered viewpoints while underrepresenting less mainstream but potentially valid perspectives.
- **Survivorship bias.** Focusing on successful cases and ignoring failures when discussing strategies, companies, or technologies.

### How to Mitigate

- **Specify the perspective you want.** "Include perspectives from developing countries" or "What do critics of this approach say?"
- **Ask for dissenting views explicitly.** "What are the strongest arguments against this position?"
- **Use Model Council** to see if different models exhibit different biases on the same topic.
- **Be aware of your own biases.** If a response confirms what you already believed, verify it more rigorously, not less.

---

## Inability to Access Certain Content

Perplexity cannot access:

- **Paywalled content.** Newspapers, journals, and databases behind subscription walls.
- **Private or internal content.** Your company's intranet, private Slack messages, or internal databases (unless you upload them).
- **App-only content.** Information that exists only within mobile apps or walled platforms.

- **Very new content.** Pages that have not yet been indexed.
- **Blocked content.** Websites that block AI crawlers.

This creates systematic blind spots. If the best information on your topic lives behind a paywall, Perplexity will give you a response based on whatever free sources it can find — which may be inferior.

### How to Mitigate

- **Supplement with your own access.** If you have subscriptions to relevant journals, databases, or news sources, use them alongside Perplexity.
- **Upload paywalled documents.** If you have legitimate access to a paywalled article, download it and upload it to Perplexity for analysis.
- **Recognize the gaps.** When Perplexity's response on a topic feels thin, consider whether the best sources might be behind walls it cannot access.

---

## Oversimplification

When asked about complex topics, the AI tends to present a cleaner, simpler version of reality than actually exists. Nuances flatten, exceptions get omitted, multi-dimensional issues collapse into simple narratives.

This is partly by design (clear, readable responses) and partly a limitation (the model may not capture the full complexity of certain topics). It can be dangerous when the nuances matter.

### How to Mitigate

- **Ask for nuance explicitly.** "What are the exceptions to this general rule?" or "Where does this explanation break down?"
- **Ask for competing interpretations.** "What do different schools of thought say about this?"
- **Use Deep Research** for topics where oversimplification could lead to poor decisions.

---

## Formatting Hallucinations

A less-discussed failure mode: the AI sometimes generates formatting artifacts that look like real content but are not. For example:

- Fake table data that looks structured but contains invented numbers.
- Fake code that looks syntactically correct but does not compile or contains logical errors.
- Fake citations that look like real URLs but lead nowhere.

### How to Mitigate

- **Test code before using it.** Never deploy AI-generated code without running and testing it.
- **Click citations.** Verify that cited URLs actually exist and contain the claimed content.
- **Spot-check data.** If the AI generates a table of data, verify a few data points against primary sources.

---

## What to Do When Perplexity Gets It Wrong

When you catch an error:

1. **Do not assume the entire response is wrong.** A response can be mostly accurate with one or two incorrect claims. Evaluate each claim individually.
2. **Ask for correction.** "The statistic you cited about X seems incorrect based on my reading of the original source. Can you re-examine this?"
3. **Provide the correct information.** "According to the WHO, the actual figure is Y, not X as you stated. Please revise your analysis."
4. **Start a new thread if needed.** If the errors have compounded and the thread context is contaminated, a fresh start may produce better results.
5. **Report the issue.** If you find a consistently reproducible error, Perplexity's feedback mechanisms help improve the system for everyone.

---

## A Healthy Relationship with AI Search

The goal is not to distrust Perplexity. It is to trust it appropriately. For everyday queries — factual lookups, concept explanations, overview research, and brainstorming — Perplexity earns its keep. The failure modes catalogued in this chapter are real, but they cluster around specific situations: high-stakes decisions, detailed quantitative analysis, fast-moving events, and topics where the best sources are not freely available online. In those cases, treat Perplexity as a starting point and verify independently.

The users who get the most value from Perplexity are not the ones who trust it blindly or the ones who distrust it entirely. They are the ones with calibrated expectations: they know what it does well, they know where it stumbles, and they verify when the stakes are high.

---

## Chapter Summary

Perplexity's main failure modes include hallucination, source quality issues, recency gaps, reasoning errors, context window limitations, bias, inability to access certain content, and oversimplification. None of these are unique to Perplexity — they are inherent to current AI systems — but understanding them is essential for using the tool responsibly. The antidotes are the same throughout: check citations, cross-reference important claims, ask for nuance and dissenting views, verify quantitative data, and treat AI output as a starting point for your own critical thinking.

# Chapter 24: Privacy, Security, and Safe Use

## Protecting Yourself While Using AI Search

Every time you type a query into Perplexity, you share information. Sometimes that information is trivial – "What time does the pharmacy close?" reveals little about you. But other queries can be deeply personal: health concerns, financial situations, legal troubles, relationship problems, political views, or business secrets.

Understanding what happens to your data, how to protect yourself, and how to make informed decisions about what to share is not optional. It is a core part of using any AI tool responsibly.

---

## What Data Does Perplexity Collect?

When you use Perplexity, the following data points may be collected:

- **Your queries.** Every question you ask.
- **Your uploaded files.** Documents, images, and spreadsheets you upload for analysis.
- **Your account information.** Email, name, payment details for subscribers.
- **Usage data.** Which features you use, how often, timestamps, device information.
- **Conversation history.** The full threads of your interactions.

The exact data practices depend on your plan tier and Perplexity's current terms of service and privacy policy. These documents evolve, so check the current versions periodically.

### Free vs. Pro vs. Enterprise

Data handling typically differs by tier:

- **Free tier.** Generally the least data protection. Queries and interactions may be used to improve the service, including model training.
- **Enterprise tier.** Typically includes the strongest guarantees: no use of data for training, data isolation, compliance certifications, and admin controls over data retention and access.

If your privacy needs are high, the enterprise tier's contractual data protections are worth the investment.

---

## What You Should Not Share

Regardless of your plan tier, exercise judgment about what you type into any AI tool:

### Personal Identifiers

Do not include Social Security numbers, passport numbers, driver's license numbers, or other government-issued identifiers in your queries. Perplexity does not need these, and including them creates unnecessary risk.

### Passwords and Credentials

Never paste passwords, API keys, private encryption keys, or authentication tokens into a Perplexity query. If you are asking about a security issue, describe the problem without including actual credentials.

### Sensitive Personal Information

Medical diagnoses, mental health details, sexual orientation, religious beliefs, political affiliations — think carefully before including these in queries. Perplexity is a useful research tool for sensitive topics, but consider whether you need to include personal details or whether you can phrase the query in the third person or hypothetically.

### Confidential Business Information

Trade secrets, unreleased product plans, internal financial data, confidential legal matters, and customer data should not be shared with Perplexity on non-enterprise plans. If you must research sensitive business topics, use an enterprise plan with appropriate data protections — or phrase your queries in generic terms that do not reveal specifics.

### Other People's Information

Do not share other people's personal data (addresses, phone numbers, financial information, health details) without their consent. This is both an ethical obligation and, in many jurisdictions, a legal one.

---

## Privacy Settings and Controls

Perplexity offers several privacy-related settings. Familiarize yourself with them:

### Conversation History

You can typically control whether your conversation history is saved. Turning off history means your queries are not stored in your account for later reference — but check whether they are still processed or retained temporarily server-side.

### Data Deletion

Most AI platforms, including Perplexity, let you delete your data — individual conversations, uploaded files, or your entire account. Familiarize yourself with the deletion process and understand its scope: does deletion remove the data from backups? How long does it take to propagate?

### Account Security

Protect your Perplexity account with strong security practices:

- Use a strong, unique password.
- Enable two-factor authentication if available.
- Do not share your account credentials.

- Log out on shared devices.
- Review your account activity periodically for unauthorized access.

---

## Data Jurisdiction and Compliance

Where your data is stored and processed matters, especially for business users:

- **GDPR.** If you are in the European Union or handle EU residents' data, ensure your use of Perplexity complies with GDPR requirements, including data processing agreements, data transfer mechanisms, and data subject rights.
- **CCPA.** California residents have specific rights regarding their personal information. Understand how Perplexity handles CCPA requests.
- **Industry regulations.** Healthcare (HIPAA), finance (SOX, PCI-DSS), education (FERPA), and other regulated industries have specific data handling requirements. Make sure your use of Perplexity does not create compliance violations.
- **Data residency.** Some organizations require that data be stored in specific geographic regions. Check whether Perplexity can meet data residency requirements.

For regulated industries and organizations with strict compliance requirements, the enterprise plan — with its contractual guarantees and compliance certifications — is usually the minimum viable option.

---

## Secure Browsing with Comet

If you use the Comet Browser (Chapter 15), additional privacy considerations apply:

- **On-page AI processing.** When you use AI features on a web page, the page content is sent to Perplexity's servers for analysis. Keep this in mind when browsing sensitive pages.
- **Browsing data.** Understand what browsing data Comet collects and syncs. Review the privacy settings and adjust them to your comfort level.

- **Private browsing mode.** Use Comet's private browsing mode for sessions where you want minimal data collection.

---

## File Upload Security

When you upload files to Perplexity:

- **Understand what happens to the file.** Is it stored permanently? Is it processed and then deleted? Is it encrypted at rest?
- **Strip metadata before uploading.** Documents and images can contain metadata (author name, GPS coordinates, revision history) you may not want to share. Use metadata removal tools before uploading sensitive files.
- **Do not upload files containing other people's sensitive data** unless you have authorization and appropriate data protections in place.
- **Use Spaces with file sync cautiously.** Enterprise file sync connects Perplexity to your cloud storage. Limit the sync scope to the folders you intend to share, not your entire drive.

---

## Safe Research Practices

### Sensitive Health Research

If you are researching a health condition — yours or someone else's — you can use Perplexity well without exposing personal details:

- Instead of: "I was diagnosed with stage 2 breast cancer. What are my treatment options?"
- Try: "What are the current treatment options for stage 2 breast cancer, and what factors influence the choice between them?"

The second query gets you the same information without disclosing personal medical data.

### Legal Research

When researching legal matters:

- Do not include case-specific details that could identify the parties involved.
- Phrase queries in hypothetical terms: "In a situation where an employer terminates an employee for X reason in California, what legal protections apply?"
- Consult an actual lawyer for legal advice. Perplexity is a research tool, not legal counsel.

### Financial Research

When researching financial topics:

- Do not share your actual account numbers, balances, or portfolio details.
- Use hypothetical scenarios: "If someone had $200,000 in a traditional IRA and was considering a Roth conversion, what would the tax implications be?"
- Verify financial information against authoritative sources (IRS, SEC, established financial institutions).

---

## Children and Minors

If you are a parent, educator, or guardian:

- Be aware that Perplexity's terms of service typically specify a minimum age for account creation.
- Supervise children's use of AI tools.
- Teach children not to share personal information (name, school, address, age) with AI tools.
- Use parental controls and content filters where available.

---

## Emerging Threats

The intersection of AI and privacy creates new categories of risk:

### Prompt Injection

Malicious content on the web can influence AI responses. If a website contains hidden instructions designed to manipulate AI systems, Perplexity could incorporate those instructions when processing the page. This is an evolving area of AI security research.

### Social Engineering

AI tools can be used to research individuals for social engineering attacks. Information you share publicly (including through Perplexity's publicly shared Pages) can be used by bad actors to craft targeted attacks.

### Data Aggregation

Individual queries may seem harmless, but a pattern of queries over time can reveal a detailed profile of your interests, concerns, and circumstances. Consider the aggregate picture your queries paint, not just each one in isolation.

---

## A Practical Privacy Framework

For everyday Perplexity use, follow this framework:

1. **Before typing a query, ask yourself:** Does this contain personal information I would not want stored on a server I do not control?
2. **If yes, anonymize it.** Rephrase to remove personal identifiers while preserving the question's substance.
3. **For sensitive topics, use the most private settings available.** Disable history, use private browsing, or use an enterprise plan with data protections.
4. **For uploaded files, assess the sensitivity.** Public documents are fine. Confidential documents require enterprise-grade protections.
5. **Review and clean up periodically.** Delete old threads and uploaded files you no longer need.

6. **Stay informed.** Privacy policies change. Check Perplexity's current policies at least once a year.

---

## Chapter Summary

Privacy with Perplexity requires conscious choices. Understand what data is collected, control what you share, use appropriate plan tiers for sensitive work, anonymize personal queries, protect your account, and stay aware of jurisdiction-specific compliance requirements. The tool is powerful, and the privacy tradeoffs are manageable — but only if you manage them actively. Default settings are not always the most private, and your comfort with data sharing should guide your usage patterns.

# Chapter 25: The Ethics of AI-Powered Search

## Searching Responsibly in the Age of AI

Perplexity is not just a tool. It is part of a larger transformation in how humanity finds, processes, and acts on information. That transformation raises ethical questions you — as a user — cannot entirely outsource to the company that built the platform. How you use AI-powered search has consequences: for yourself, for the people whose content you consume, for the accuracy of public discourse, and for the viability of the information ecosystem that makes the tool work in the first place.

This chapter addresses those ethical dimensions head-on, not with lectures but with practical frameworks for making good choices.

---

## The Publisher Problem

This is the foundational ethical tension of AI-powered search: Perplexity generates answers by drawing on content created by journalists, researchers, bloggers, and other publishers. When the AI gives you a comprehensive answer with citations, you may never visit the source. The publisher created the value; the AI platform (and you) captured it.

### Why This Matters

Publishing is a business. Journalists need salaries. Research institutions need funding. Bloggers and independent analysts need income to keep creating. If the economic model that supports content creation collapses, the quality and quantity of available information declines — which eventually degrades the AI itself.

### What Perplexity Is Doing About It

Perplexity has taken several steps to address this tension:

- **Abandoning ads.** In February 2026, Perplexity abandoned its advertising model, removing a major source of friction with publishers who objected to their content being monetized through ads they had no part in.
- **Comet Plus publisher revenue sharing.** The Comet Plus subscription ($5/month) directs a portion of revenue to the publishers whose content users interact with. This creates a direct economic link between content consumption and compensation.
- **Citations.** Every Perplexity response includes citations linking to the original sources, giving publishers attribution and potential click-through traffic.

### What You Can Do

- **Click through to sources.** When Perplexity cites an article that was useful to you, visit the original. This generates traffic and advertising revenue (where applicable) for the publisher.
- **Subscribe to Comet Plus.** If you use Comet Browser, the $5 per month subscription compensates the publishers whose work informs your research.
- **Support publishers directly.** Subscribe to news outlets, journals, and independent creators whose work you value. Perplexity makes their content more accessible to you; returning some of that value is the right thing to do.
- **Share original sources, not just AI summaries.** When you share information with others, link to the original article or paper, not just your Perplexity thread.

---

## Accuracy and the Spread of Misinformation

AI-powered search can either help or harm the accuracy of public discourse, depending on how it is used.

### The Good

Perplexity's citation model is more transparent than a traditional chatbot. When every claim comes with a source link, you can verify. This is a meaningful improvement over AI tools that make claims without attribution.

### The Risk

The risk emerges when users treat AI-generated answers as authoritative without checking the citations. An incorrect but well-formatted, confidently stated response spreads if someone copies it into a report, shares it on social media, or uses it to make a decision.

### Your Responsibility

- **Verify before sharing.** If you are going to share AI-generated information with others, verify it first — especially factual claims, statistics, and quotes.
- **Disclose the source.** When you share AI-assisted research, be transparent that you used an AI tool. This lets your audience apply appropriate scrutiny.
- **Do not present AI output as your own expertise.** Using Perplexity to research a topic is legitimate. Presenting yourself as an expert on a topic you only read an AI summary about is not.
- **Correct errors publicly.** If you share information that turns out to be wrong, correct it with the same visibility you gave the original claim.

---

## Academic and Professional Integrity

We covered academic integrity in Chapter 20, but the ethical dimension deserves emphasis here.

### The Core Principle

Using AI to research is different from using AI to produce. Researching a topic with Perplexity and then writing your own analysis is honest work. Submitting AI-generated text as your own — whether in academia, journalism, or professional settings — is dishonest.

The line between the two is not always sharp. A spectrum runs from "I used Perplexity to find relevant papers" (clearly fine) through "I asked Perplexity to outline my paper" (gray area) to "I asked Perplexity to write my paper and submitted it as mine" (clearly wrong). Each person needs to place themselves on this spectrum honestly, guided by their institution's policies and their own integrity.

### Disclosure Norms

Norms around AI disclosure are still forming. In many contexts, using AI tools for research is expected and unremarkable — as using a search engine has been for decades. In other contexts (academic submissions, journalism, legal filings), disclosure of AI assistance may be required or advisable.

When in doubt, disclose. Transparency never hurts your credibility; concealment, once discovered, always does.

---

## Bias and Representation

AI systems reflect the data they are trained on and the sources they search. They can perpetuate and amplify existing biases:

- **Whose knowledge counts?** If the AI primarily draws on English-language, Western-centric sources, it presents a skewed view of many global topics.
- **Whose perspectives are centered?** Majority viewpoints tend to be overrepresented. Minority perspectives may be underrepresented or presented as fringe.
- **What is considered neutral?** The AI's presentation of "balanced" information reflects the biases of its training data, not an objectively neutral position.

### What You Can Do

- **Seek diverse perspectives.** Ask Perplexity specifically for perspectives from underrepresented groups, developing countries, non-English sources, or minority viewpoints.

- **Question "default" framing.** When the AI presents something as normal, standard, or mainstream, ask yourself: for whom? Where? According to whom?
- **Recognize what is missing.** The absence of a perspective in an AI response does not mean that perspective does not exist or is not valid. It may mean the AI's sources are limited.

---

## Environmental Impact

AI search consumes far more computational resources than traditional search. Every Perplexity query involves running large language models, executing web searches, and processing the results. Deep Research queries are especially resource-intensive.

The environmental cost of this computation — primarily energy consumption and associated carbon emissions — is real. It is not a reason to stop using AI search, but it is a reason to use it thoughtfully.

### What You Can Do

- **Do not use Deep Research for trivial questions.** Match the tool to the task. A simple factual question does not need a multi-step investigation.
- **Be efficient with your queries.** Well-crafted queries that land on the first try consume fewer resources than poorly crafted ones that require multiple iterations.
- **Support companies that invest in sustainable computing.** As a consumer and voter, favor AI companies that use renewable energy and invest in reducing the environmental impact of their infrastructure.

---

## Power Imbalances

AI tools like Perplexity are not equally accessible to everyone:

- **Cost.** Pro and Max subscriptions give paying users access to more powerful features. Free-tier users get a limited experience.

- **Digital literacy.** Users who understand how to prompt effectively get dramatically better results than those who do not.
- **Language.** Perplexity works best in English. Users of other languages may get lower-quality results.
- **Access.** People without reliable internet, modern devices, or technological familiarity are excluded entirely.

These imbalances are not unique to Perplexity, but they are worth acknowledging. If you can share knowledge about effective AI use with others — colleagues, students, community members — doing so helps level the playing field.

---

## The Automation of Judgment

Perhaps the deepest ethical question about AI search is this: as AI gets better at finding, synthesizing, and presenting information, are we losing our capacity for independent judgment?

When Perplexity gives you a well-structured, well-cited answer, the temptation is to accept it and move on. The answer looks right, it has sources, and checking independently takes time you do not have. Over hundreds of queries, you build a habit of deference.

This is a personal choice, not a policy question. But consider the long-term implications: outsourcing judgment to AI systems creates real risks — errors that scale, manipulation, and atrophy of critical thinking.

### Maintaining Your Intellectual Independence

- **Use AI to inform, not to decide.** Let Perplexity provide information and analysis. Make the decision yourself.
- **Practice disagreeing with the AI.** Sometimes argue against the AI's conclusion — even if you ultimately agree with it. This keeps your critical thinking muscles active.
- **Read primary sources.** Do not let AI summaries be your only engagement with important topics. Read the original articles, papers, and data.

- **Form opinions before searching.** On topics you have some knowledge of, form a preliminary opinion before asking Perplexity. Then see how the AI's response challenges, confirms, or nuances your thinking. This is more intellectually honest than starting with no position and adopting whatever the AI says.

---

## An Ethical Framework for AI Search Use

Here is a practical framework you can apply:

1. **Am I being honest?** Am I using AI output transparently, or am I misrepresenting AI work as my own?
2. **Am I being fair?** Am I supporting the creators whose work makes AI possible? Am I considering perspectives beyond what the AI defaults to?
3. **Am I being careful?** Am I verifying important claims? Am I thinking critically about the AI's output?
4. **Am I being proportionate?** Am I using the right level of tool for the task? Am I consuming resources thoughtfully?
5. **Am I maintaining my agency?** Am I using AI to augment my thinking, or am I letting it replace my thinking?

---

## Chapter Summary

AI-powered search is not ethically neutral. It raises questions about publisher compensation, misinformation, academic integrity, bias, environmental impact, and the automation of judgment. As a user, you have both the ability and the responsibility to navigate these questions thoughtfully. Support publishers, verify before sharing, disclose AI usage, seek diverse perspectives, use resources proportionally, and protect your intellectual independence. The technology is powerful. How you wield it is up to you.

# Part VIII: Reference

*"Knowledge is of two kinds. We know a subject ourselves, or we know where we can find information upon it."*

— Samuel Johnson

# Chapter 26: Epilogue — Where You Go from Here

You have covered a lot of ground.

You started by understanding what Perplexity is and why it exists. You chose a plan, set up the tool on your devices, and learned how to craft searches that get real answers instead of lists of links. You explored Focus modes, Spaces, Pages, Deep Research, file uploads, image generation, the Comet Browser, and Model Council. You learned how to apply these tools as a student, a professional, a team leader, and a developer. And you spent time thinking critically about what AI-powered search gets wrong, how to protect your privacy, and the ethical questions that come with this technology.

That is a solid foundation. A foundation is only useful if you build on it.

The gap between knowing how a tool works and using it instinctively closes through one thing: daily practice. Make Perplexity part of your routine. The next time you have a question — any question, about anything — open Perplexity instead of reaching for your usual search engine. Try Pro Search on something you would normally use basic search for. Launch a Deep Research query on a topic you care about and read the full report. Set up a Space for a project you are working on right now. Experiment with a model you have not tried yet.

The more you use it, the sharper your instinct becomes for which tool fits which question. That instinct is the real skill this book was designed to help you build.

AI-powered search is still young. Perplexity will look different six months from now — new features, new models, new capabilities none of us can fully predict. The fundamentals you have learned here will carry forward, but the details will evolve. Stay curious. Check the Perplexity blog. Revisit features you skimmed over the first time. And if you are ready for more, the companion volume — *Perplexity AI: The Advanced Research Playbook (2026 Edition)* — covers advanced prompting, API development, enterprise workflows, and the techniques that separate casual users from power users.

Thank you for reading. Now go search for something that matters to you.

The search bar is waiting.

# Appendix A: Quick Tips and Cheat Sheet

## Your At-a-Glance Reference for Perplexity

This appendix distills the book's advice into a fast-reference format. Pin it, print it, or bookmark it for quick access while you work.

---

## Query Writing Essentials

- **Use full sentences, not keywords.** "What is the best lightweight laptop for programming in 2026?" beats "best laptop programming 2026."
- **Include context.** State your role, background, or situation: "As a small business owner with ten employees..."
- **Set constraints.** "Only peer-reviewed sources after 2023" or "Focus on the European market."
- **Define criteria.** "Prioritize reliability over price" or "Rank by ease of implementation."
- **Specify the format.** "Give me a comparison table" or "Answer in three bullet points."
- **Front-load the important details.** Put your core question first, then add context and constraints. This mirrors how the AI processes your input.
- **One topic per query.** If you have unrelated questions, use separate threads.

---

## Format Shortcuts

| You Need | Ask For |
|---|---|
| Quick summary | "Summarize in three sentences." |
| Scannable list | "Give me a bulleted list of..." |

| You Need | Ask For |
|---|---|
| Side-by-side comparison | "Present as a comparison table with columns for X, Y, Z." |
| Step-by-step guide | "Walk me through this step by step." |
| Slide content | "Format as five slides with titles and bullet points." |
| Executive summary | "Write a one-page executive briefing with headings." |
| Data output | "Return the results as JSON" or "Format as CSV." |
| Pros and cons | "List the pros and cons in two columns." |
| Timeline | "Present the key events in chronological order." |
| Decision matrix | "Create a decision matrix scoring each option on [criteria]." |

## Feature Quick Reference

| Feature | What It Does | When to Use It |
|---|---|---|
| **Standard Search** | Fast AI-powered web search with citations | Quick factual questions, everyday research |
| **Pro Search** | Multi-step search with clarifying questions | Complex queries, comparisons, deep dives |
| **Spaces** | Persistent workspaces with custom instructions and files | Ongoing projects, team collaboration |
| **Pages** | Structured shareable reports from your research | Briefings, summaries, deliverables |
| **Deep Research** | Multi-step investigation producing reports, presentations, spreadsheets, dashboards, websites | Complex analysis, due diligence, comprehensive reports |
| **File Upload** | Upload PDFs, docs, images, spreadsheets for AI analysis | Analyzing private documents, comparing files |

| Feature | What It Does | When to Use It |
|---|---|---|
| **Image Generation** | Create images from text descriptions (Pro/Max) | Content creation, concept visualization |
| **Comet Browser** | AI-native web browser with on-page assistance | AI-enhanced daily browsing, research |
| **Comet Plus** | Enhanced Comet features + publisher revenue sharing ($5/mo) | Supporting publishers, premium browsing |
| **Model Council** | Query multiple AI models simultaneously | Complex analysis, verifying answers, creative work |

---

## Focus Modes

- **Web** — Default. Broad web search. Use for general questions.
- **Academic** — Scholarly sources and journals. Use for research and evidence-based queries.
- **Video** — Video content and summaries. Use for tutorials, lectures, reviews.
- **Social** — Community discussions and real-world experiences. Use for opinions and troubleshooting.
- **Writing** — Content generation over search. Use for drafts, outlines, and creative text.
- **Finance** — SEC filings, earnings calls, corporate data. Use for company and market research.

---

## Interface Tips

- **Slash shortcut.** Press / from the home screen to jump straight to the search bar.
- **New thread shortcut.** Use `Ctrl+N` (or `Cmd+N` on Mac) to start a fresh thread without reaching for the mouse.
- **Copy responses.** Click the copy button on any response to grab the full text with formatting intact.

- **Edit your query.** If a response misses the mark, click the edit icon on your original query to revise it rather than writing a new follow-up. This reruns the search with your revised wording.
- **Share a thread.** Use the share button to generate a public link to any thread. Useful for sending research to a colleague.
- **Pin important threads.** Pin threads you return to frequently so they stay at the top of your library.
- **Collapse sources.** Click the source panel to collapse it when you want to focus on the answer text.
- **Dark mode.** Toggle dark mode in settings to reduce eye strain during long research sessions.
- **Switch models mid-thread.** On Pro and Max plans, you can change the underlying model between queries in the same thread if one model is not giving you what you need.

---

## Mobile-Specific Tips

- **Use the mobile app, not the browser.** The dedicated Perplexity app (iOS and Android) is faster, supports push notifications for shared Spaces, and handles file uploads more reliably than the mobile web version.
- **Voice input.** Tap the microphone icon to dictate your query. Useful for long, context-rich questions that are tedious to type on a phone keyboard.
- **Share to Perplexity.** On both iOS and Android, use the system share sheet to send a URL, image, or text selection directly to Perplexity for analysis. This saves you from copying and pasting.
- **Widget.** Add the Perplexity widget to your home screen for one-tap access to a new search.
- **Offline access.** You cannot run new searches offline, but previously loaded threads remain accessible if they are still in your cache. Pin important threads before you travel.
- **Quick switch.** Swipe between threads in the mobile app instead of navigating back to the library each time.

---

## Advanced Prompting Techniques

- **Role assignment:** "As a patent attorney, evaluate..."
- **Chain-of-thought:** "Think through this step by step..."
- **Negative instructions:** "Do not include anecdotal evidence..."
- **Constraint stacking:** Combine multiple filters in one query.
- **Counterargument request:** "Now argue the opposite position."
- **Gap identification:** "What important aspects have we not covered?"
- **Specificity escalation:** Start general, then ask progressively more detailed follow-ups.
- **Source steering:** "Prefer primary sources over news coverage" or "Cite only government data."

---

## Research Workflow Patterns

### The Funnel

Start broad, narrow progressively with each follow-up.

### The Debate

Research strongest arguments for, then against, then responses to objections.

### The Triangulation

Approach the same question from academic, practical, and expert-opinion angles.

### The Expert Panel

Ask the same question from multiple role perspectives (economist, engineer, ethicist).

### The Verification Loop

Get an answer, then ask Perplexity to find evidence that contradicts its own response. Reconcile the two.

---

## Power-User Habits

- **Set up Spaces for recurring projects.** Stop re-explaining context. Write custom instructions once and every query in that Space benefits.
- **Check citations before sharing.** Click through to at least two or three sources on any answer you plan to share with others. Thirty seconds of effort prevents embarrassment.
- **Use Deep Research sparingly.** Reserve it for complex investigations. For simple questions, standard or Pro Search is faster and costs fewer credits.
- **Review suggested follow-ups.** Even if you do not click them, the suggested follow-up questions can reveal angles you had not considered.
- **Delete old threads periodically.** A cluttered library makes it harder to find what you need. Archive or delete threads you are done with.
- **Pair Focus modes with follow-ups.** Start with Web Focus for an overview, then switch to Academic Focus in a follow-up to find the underlying research.
- **Export your work.** When a thread produces something valuable, export or copy it immediately. Do not assume you will find it later.

---

## Common Mistakes to Avoid

- Being too broad or vague.
- Not providing context about your situation.
- Asking multiple unrelated questions in one query.
- Trusting AI output without checking citations.
- Using Deep Research for simple factual questions.
- Sharing sensitive personal or business information on non-enterprise plans.
- Submitting AI-generated text as your own work.
- Staying on Web Focus when Academic, Finance, or Social would give better results.
- Starting a new thread when a follow-up in the same thread would be more effective (and vice versa).

## Keyboard Shortcuts and Time-Savers

- Start a new thread for new topics — do not let long threads degrade quality.
- Use Spaces with custom instructions instead of repeating context every time.
- Use follow-up questions in the same thread for iterative research.
- Bookmark or save formatting templates you use frequently.
- Use the suggested follow-up questions Perplexity offers — they surface useful angles.
- Learn the keyboard shortcuts for your platform (see Interface Tips above) to stay in flow.

---

## Privacy Checklist

- ☐ Review Perplexity's current privacy policy.
- ☐ Enable two-factor authentication on your account.
- ☐ Do not include personal identifiers in queries.
- ☐ Do not paste passwords or API keys into queries.
- ☐ Use enterprise plans for confidential business research.
- ☐ Strip metadata from sensitive files before uploading.
- ☐ Periodically delete old threads and files you no longer need.

---

## Sonar API Models at a Glance

| Model | Speed | Depth | Best For |
|---|---|---|---|
| sonar | Fast | Standard | Quick queries, high-volume apps |
| sonar-pro | Moderate | High | Detailed analysis, quality-focused apps |

| Model | Speed | Depth | Best For |
| --- | --- | --- | --- |
| sonar-reasoning-pro | Slower | Very High | Complex reasoning, professional tools |
| sonar-deep-research | Slow | Comprehensive | Full research reports, due diligence |

---

## Ethical Use Reminders

- Click through to cited sources to support publishers.
- Verify important claims before sharing.
- Disclose AI usage when appropriate.
- Seek diverse perspectives — do not lean on AI defaults.
- Use AI to inform your thinking, not replace it.

---

*This appendix is a companion to the full chapters. For detailed explanations and examples, refer to the relevant chapter.*

# Appendix B: Search Templates

## 60+ Ready-to-Use Perplexity Query Templates

Copy, customize, and use these templates as starting points for your own research. Replace the bracketed placeholders with your specific details.

---

## General Research

**1. Topic Overview** "Give me a comprehensive overview of [topic], including its history, current state, key players, and future outlook. Organize with clear headings."

**2. Pros and Cons Analysis** "What are the pros and cons of [topic/decision/technology]? Present as a two-column table with at least five items per side."

**3. Concept Explanation** "Explain [concept] in plain language. Start with a one-sentence definition, then provide a real-world analogy, then a detailed explanation, then common misconceptions."

**4. Comparison** "Compare [Option A] and [Option B] in a table with rows for: [criterion 1], [criterion 2], [criterion 3], [criterion 4], and [criterion 5]. Include a recommendation at the bottom."

**5. Timeline** "Create a timeline of the most important events in the history of [topic], from [start date] to [end date]. Include dates and brief descriptions."

**6. Current State Summary** "What is the current state of [topic/industry/technology] as of [date]? Focus on recent developments, key trends, and what experts expect next."

**7. Debate Summary** "Summarize the main arguments on both sides of the debate about [topic]. What does each side get right, and where are the weaknesses in each position?"

**8. Key Statistics** "What are the most important statistics about [topic]? Give me at least ten data points with their sources and dates."

---

## Business and Market Research

**9. Market Size and Growth** "What is the current market size for [industry/product category] in [region]? What is the projected compound annual growth rate through [year]? Cite specific sources."

**10. Competitive Landscape** "Who are the top [number] competitors in the [industry] space? For each, summarize their key products, target market, strengths, weaknesses, and approximate market share."

**11. Company Research** "Provide a comprehensive overview of [company name]: founding, key products/services, revenue, number of employees, recent news, competitive positioning, and notable strengths and weaknesses."

**12. Industry Trends** "What are the five most significant trends shaping the [industry] in [year]? For each trend, explain the driving forces and potential impact."

**13. SWOT Analysis** "Create a SWOT analysis (Strengths, Weaknesses, Opportunities, Threats) for [company/product/strategy]. Present as a four-quadrant table."

**14. Pricing Research** "What are typical pricing models and price ranges for [product/service category] in the [market/region]? Include examples from leading providers."

**15. Customer Pain Points** "What are the most common pain points and complaints that [target audience] have with [product category/industry]? Draw on review sites, forums, and user feedback."

**16. Regulatory Landscape** "What regulations currently govern [industry/activity] in [country/region]? What regulatory changes are expected in [timeframe]?"

**17. Partnership/Acquisition Target Research** "Research [company name] as a potential [partnership/acquisition] target. Include financial health, product fit, cultural indicators, risks, and recent strategic moves."

**18. Meeting Prep Brief** "I have a meeting with [company name/person]. Give me a one-page briefing covering: recent company news, key leadership, products/services, market position, and potential talking points."

---

## Technology and Development

**19. Technology Comparison** "Compare [Technology A], [Technology B], and [Technology C] for [specific use case]. Create a table with rows for: performance, ease of use, community/ecosystem, learning curve, cost, and scalability."

**20. Architecture Decision** "I am building [type of application] with [constraints]. What are the tradeoffs between [architecture option A] and [architecture option B]? Consider scalability, complexity, cost, and team expertise requirements."

**21. Best Practices** "What are the current best practices for [specific technical task] in [year]? Include code examples or configuration examples where applicable."

**22. Library/Framework Evaluation** "Evaluate [library/framework name] for [use case]. Cover: features, performance, documentation quality, community size, maintenance status, and notable alternatives."

**23. Error Troubleshooting** "I am getting this error: [paste error]. My setup is [language/framework/version/OS]. What are the most likely causes and solutions?"

**24. API Integration Guide** "How do I integrate [API/service name] with [my technology stack]? Give me a step-by-step guide with code examples."

**25. Security Assessment** "What are the main security considerations for [technology/architecture/approach]? List the top vulnerabilities and recommended mitigations."

**26. Performance Optimization** "What are the most effective ways to optimize [specific aspect] performance in a [type of application] built with [technology stack]?"

---

## Academic and Learning

**27. Literature Survey** "What are the most important papers on [topic] published between [start year] and [end year]? For each, give the title, authors, publication, and a two-sentence summary of key findings."

**28. Methodology Explanation** "Explain the [research methodology] in detail. When is it appropriate to use? What are its strengths and limitations? Give an example of a well-designed study using this method."

**29. Theory Summary** "Summarize [theory name] in [field]. Who developed it? What are its core claims? What evidence supports it? What are the main criticisms?"

**30. Exam Prep Questions** "Generate [number] practice exam questions on [topic] at the [introductory/intermediate/advanced] level. Include answers and brief explanations."

**31. Concept Comparison** "Compare and contrast [concept A] and [concept B] in [field]. What do they have in common? Where do they differ? When would you use each?"

**32. Research Gap Identification** "Based on recent literature on [topic], what are the main gaps in current research? What questions remain unanswered?"

**33. Reading List** "Recommend [number] essential readings for someone getting started in [field/topic]. For each, explain why it is important and what the reader will learn."

**34. Study Guide** "Create a study guide for [course/exam/topic] covering the key concepts, important terms, and relationships between ideas. Organize by theme."

---

## Content and Marketing

**35. Blog Post Outline** "Create a detailed outline for a blog post about [topic]. Target audience: [audience]. Desired length: [word count]. Include a compelling title, introduction hook, main sections with bullet points, and a conclusion with CTA."

**36. Social Media Content Ideas** "Generate [number] social media post ideas for a [type of business] targeting [audience] on [platform]. For each, include the hook, key message, and suggested format (text, image, video, poll)."

**37. Email Newsletter Outline** "Outline a newsletter about [topic] for [audience]. Include: subject line options, introduction, main story, secondary items, and call to action."

**38. SEO Topic Research** "What are the most important subtopics and questions people are searching for related to [main topic]? Organize by search intent (informational, transactional, navigational)."

**39. Content Gap Analysis** "Analyze the content landscape for [topic/keyword]. What do the top-ranking articles cover well, and what do they miss? Where is the opportunity for new content?"

**40. Case Study Framework** "Create a framework for writing a case study about [company/project]. Include sections for: challenge, solution, implementation, results, and key takeaways."

---

## Career and Professional

**41. Salary Research** "What is the typical salary range for a [job title] in [city/region] with [years] of experience? Include data from multiple sources and note whether the figures include bonuses and equity."

**42. Job Description Analysis** "Analyze this job description: [paste job description]. What are the key skills required? What does the company seem to prioritize? What questions should I ask in an interview?"

**43. Interview Prep** "What are the most common interview questions for a [job title] role at [type of company]? For each, suggest how to structure a strong answer."

**44. Career Transition Research** "I am considering transitioning from [current role] to [target role]. What skills transfer? What gaps would I need to fill? What is a realistic timeline and path?"

**45. Industry Certification Comparison** "Compare the top certifications in [field]: [Cert A], [Cert B], [Cert C]. Include cost, time commitment, industry recognition, and career impact."

---

## Personal Finance and Decisions

**46. Product Research** "I am looking to buy [product type] with a budget of [amount]. My priorities are [priority 1], [priority 2], and [priority 3]. What are the top three options and how do they compare?"

**47. Service Comparison** "Compare [Service A], [Service B], and [Service C] for [use case]. Include pricing, features, user reviews, and any notable limitations."

**48. Investment Research** "What should I know about investing in [asset type/sector] in [year]? Cover the current market conditions, main risks, potential returns, and expert consensus."

**49. Insurance Research** "What types of [insurance category] are available in [country/state]? What does each cover? What factors affect pricing? What should I prioritize?"

**50. Major Purchase Decision** "Help me think through whether to [buy/rent/lease] [item/property]. My situation: [brief description]. What are the financial and practical considerations?"

---

## Travel and Personal

**51. Trip Planning** "Plan a [duration] trip to [destination] in [month]. I am interested in [interests]. Budget: [amount]. Include a day-by-day itinerary, accommodation suggestions, and practical tips."

**52. Restaurant Research** "What are the best [cuisine type] restaurants in [area]? Include price range, ambiance, standout dishes, and whether reservations are needed."

**53. Health Research** "What does current medical research say about [condition/treatment/supplement]? Summarize the evidence, noting the quality and quantity of studies. Include any risks or side effects."

**54. Hobby Deep Dive** "I want to get started with [hobby]. What equipment do I need? What are the basic skills to learn first? What resources (books, courses, communities) do you recommend?"

**55. Home Improvement** "What are the steps involved in [home improvement project]? Estimated cost, time, tools needed, and when to call a professional instead of DIY."

---

## Analysis and Decision-Making

**56. Risk Assessment** "What are the main risks associated with [decision/project/investment]? For each risk, rate the likelihood (low/medium/high) and potential impact (low/medium/high). Suggest mitigations."

**57. Stakeholder Analysis** "Who are the key stakeholders for [project/decision/policy]? What are their interests, concerns, and likely positions? How should each be engaged?"

**58. Cost-Benefit Analysis** "Perform a cost-benefit analysis of [proposal/project]. List tangible and intangible costs and benefits. Which factors are most uncertain?"

**59. Scenario Planning** "For [decision/situation], describe three scenarios: best case, worst case, and most likely. What would trigger each scenario, and how should I prepare for each?"

**60. Root Cause Analysis** "[Problem description]. What are the most likely root causes? Use a structured approach (e.g., 5 Whys or fishbone diagram) to identify contributing factors."

---

## Specialized Templates

**61. Grant/Funding Research** "What grants or funding opportunities are available for [type of project/organization] in [country/region]? Include eligibility requirements, amounts, and deadlines."

**62. Legal Question Research** "What are the legal considerations for [activity/business type] in [jurisdiction]? Cover relevant laws, common compliance issues, and where to find authoritative guidance."

**63. Vendor Evaluation** "Create an evaluation framework for selecting a vendor for [product/service]. Include criteria, weighting, and a scoring template. Then evaluate [Vendor A], [Vendor B], and [Vendor C] against the framework."

**64. Event Planning** "Help me plan [type of event] for [number] people in [location/month]. Include venue considerations, budget breakdown, timeline, vendor needs, and common pitfalls."

**65. Policy Analysis** "Analyze [policy name/proposal]. What problem does it address? What are the proposed mechanisms? What does evidence from similar policies elsewhere suggest about likely outcomes? What are the main objections?"

---

## How to Customize These Templates

Each template is a starting point. To get better results:

1. **Add your specific context.** Replace generic placeholders with your actual details.
2. **Adjust the scope.** Narrow or broaden as needed for your situation.

3. **Specify the format.** Add formatting instructions if the template does not include them.
4. **Layer constraints.** Add source requirements, date ranges, geographic limitations, or audience specifications.
5. **Iterate.** Use the initial response as a springboard for follow-up questions that go deeper.

---

*These templates work with standard Perplexity search, Spaces, Deep Research, and the Sonar API. Adjust complexity and depth expectations based on the feature you are using.*

# Appendix C: Troubleshooting

## Common Problems and How to Fix Them

This appendix covers the issues Perplexity users encounter most frequently, with practical solutions for each.

---

## Query and Response Issues

#### Problem: Vague or unhelpful responses

**Cause:** Your query is too broad or lacks context.

**Solution:** Add specificity. Include your context, constraints, criteria, and desired format. Compare "Tell me about marketing" with "What are the three most effective content marketing strategies for a B2B SaaS company targeting mid-market CFOs in 2026? Present as a numbered list with one paragraph per strategy."

---

#### Problem: Response does not match what you asked for

**Cause:** Ambiguous phrasing or missing context.

**Solution:** Rephrase with explicit instructions. If you asked "What about the cost?" and got a response about a different cost than you intended, specify: "What is the monthly subscription cost for [specific product], not the implementation cost?"

---

#### Problem: Response is too long

**Cause:** No length constraint in your query.

**Solution:** Add explicit length instructions: "Answer in three bullet points" or "Keep your response under 150 words."

---

#### Problem: Response is too short or superficial

**Cause:** Query was phrased as a simple question when you wanted depth.

**Solution:** Ask for detail explicitly: "Provide a detailed analysis with specific examples and data" or use Deep Research for comprehensive investigation.

---

#### Problem: Outdated information in the response

**Cause:** Sources may be old, or the topic has changed recently.

**Solution:** Add a recency constraint: "Only cite sources from the past six months" or "What is the situation as of [month/year]?" If the topic is recent, note that web sources may not yet be comprehensive.

---

#### Problem: AI seems to "forget" earlier parts of the conversation

**Cause:** Long threads can exceed the model's effective context window.

**Solution:** Start a new thread and include the key context from the earlier conversation in your first message. Alternatively, use a Space with custom instructions for persistent context.

---

#### Problem: Response contains incorrect information

**Cause:** Hallucination, misinterpretation of sources, or low-quality source material.

**Solution:** Check the citations. Point out the error: "The statistic you cited appears to be incorrect. According to [source], the actual figure is X. Please revise." For critical research, use Model Council to cross-reference multiple models.

---

## Feature-Specific Issues

### Problem: Uploaded file is not being analyzed correctly

**Causes:** - File is too large. - File is a scanned PDF with poor image quality. - File has complex formatting (merged cells, embedded images, nested tables).

**Solutions:** - For large files, ask about specific sections rather than requesting analysis of the entire document. - For scanned PDFs, try to obtain a text-based version or a higher-quality scan. - For complex spreadsheets, clean the data (remove merged cells, add column headers, eliminate empty rows) before uploading.

---

### Problem: Deep Research is taking too long

**Cause:** Deep Research is computationally intensive by design and can take several minutes.

**Solution:** This is normal behavior, not a problem. Wait for it to complete. If it stalls for an unusually long time (more than ten minutes), try refreshing or resubmitting. For less complex questions, use standard search or Pages instead.

---

### Problem: Space custom instructions are not being followed

**Causes:** - Instructions are vague or contradictory. - Instructions conflict with the specific query. - Instructions exceed the character limit and are being truncated.

**Solutions:** - Rewrite instructions to be specific and unambiguous. - Check for contradictions (e.g., "Be concise" and "Provide detailed analysis" in the same instructions). - If instructions are long, prioritize the most important directives at the top.

---

### Problem: Image generation produces poor results

**Cause:** Vague or insufficient prompt.

**Solutions:** - Add detail: describe the subject, style, setting, lighting, composition, and mood. - Iterate: refine the prompt based on what the first result got wrong. - See Chapter 14 for detailed guidance on crafting image generation prompts.

---

#### Problem: Model Council responses all look the same

**Cause:** The question may be straightforward enough that all models agree.

**Solution:** This is a good sign — it means there is strong consensus. Model Council is most useful for ambiguous, analytical, or creative questions where models diverge. For simple factual queries, similar responses indicate reliability.

---

## Account and Access Issues

#### Problem: Features are grayed out or unavailable

**Cause:** Your plan tier does not include that feature.

**Solution:** Check which features are included in your plan (Free, Pro, Max, Enterprise). Deep Research, image generation, and some advanced features require Pro or higher.

---

#### Problem: Hit usage limits

**Cause:** Each plan tier has daily or monthly limits on certain features.

**Solution:** Wait for the limit to reset (usually daily), upgrade your plan for higher limits, or use standard search instead of premium features for less critical queries.

---

#### Problem: Cannot access Perplexity at all

**Causes:** - Internet connectivity issue. - Perplexity service outage. - Account issue (suspended, billing problem). - Network or firewall blocking.

**Solutions:** - Check your internet connection. - Check Perplexity's status page or social media for service outage announcements. - Log in from a different device or network to isolate the issue. - Check your account status and billing information. - If on a corporate network, check whether your IT department blocks AI tools.

---

## Performance Tips

### Getting Faster Responses

- Use the standard sonar model for quick queries instead of pro or reasoning models.
- Keep queries concise and well-structured — less parsing, faster processing.
- Avoid uploading unnecessarily large files.

### Getting Higher Quality Responses

- Use sonar-pro or Deep Research for important questions.
- Provide rich context in your queries.
- Use follow-up questions to refine and deepen the initial response.
- Use Model Council for questions where accuracy matters.

### Reducing Costs (API Users)

- Choose the lightest model that meets your quality requirements.
- Implement response caching for repeated queries.
- Set appropriate max_tokens limits.
- Monitor usage to catch unexpected spikes.

---

## When to Contact Support

Contact Perplexity support if:

- You experience a persistent technical issue that the troubleshooting steps above do not resolve.
- You believe your account has been compromised.

- You encounter billing errors.
- You need enterprise-specific assistance (data protection, compliance, team administration).
- You have found a reproducible bug that should be reported.

---

*For the latest troubleshooting information, check Perplexity's help center and community forums, which are updated more frequently than any printed guide.*

# Appendix D: Glossary

## Key Terms for Perplexity and AI-Powered Search

This glossary defines the terms you will encounter throughout this book and in your use of Perplexity. Terms are listed alphabetically.

---

**Academic Focus** — A Focus mode that restricts Perplexity's sources to scholarly papers, peer-reviewed journals, and research databases. Best for evidence-based queries and literature reviews.

**Agentic AI** — AI that can take autonomous, multi-step actions to complete a task, rather than simply answering a single question. Perplexity Computer is an example of agentic AI.

**API (Application Programming Interface)** — A set of rules and protocols that allows software applications to communicate with each other. The Sonar API lets developers integrate Perplexity's capabilities into their own applications.

**Chain-of-thought prompting** — A technique where you ask the AI to show its reasoning step by step, rather than jumping directly to a conclusion. Produces more thorough and transparent responses.

**Citation** — A reference to the source of information. Perplexity includes citations (typically as numbered links to web pages) in every response, allowing you to verify claims against their original sources. Citations are the primary mechanism for grounding Perplexity's answers in verifiable evidence.

**Comet Browser** — Perplexity's AI-native web browser, designed with AI features integrated into the core browsing experience rather than added as extensions. Free to use, with an optional paid tier.

**Comet Plus** — A $5/month subscription tier for Comet Browser that provides enhanced features and directs a portion of revenue to the publishers whose content users browse. Perplexity's approach to solving the publisher revenue-sharing problem.

**Context window** — The amount of text (measured in tokens) that an AI model can process in a single interaction. Longer context windows allow the model to consider more information, but performance may degrade toward the edges of the window.

**Custom instructions** — Persistent directives set within a Space that shape how Perplexity responds to every query in that Space. Used to define tone, format, focus areas, and constraints.

**Deep Research** — Perplexity's most thorough investigation mode. It breaks complex queries into sub-questions, conducts multi-step searches, and produces comprehensive outputs including reports, presentations, spreadsheets, dashboards, and websites. Available to Pro, Max, and Enterprise users.

**Enterprise file sync** — A feature on Perplexity's enterprise plan that automatically synchronizes files from cloud storage services (Google Drive, SharePoint, Dropbox, OneDrive, Box) with Spaces, keeping uploaded documents current.

**Enterprise Max** — Perplexity's top-tier enterprise plan at $325/seat/month, offering unlimited research queries, access to the most advanced models, and up to 10,000 files per user repository.

**Enterprise Pro** — Perplexity's business plan at $40/seat/month, offering SSO, admin controls, data privacy guarantees, and per-seat licensing for teams and organizations.

**Finance Focus** — A Focus mode that draws from SEC filings, corporate disclosures, earnings transcripts, and financial databases. Designed for investment research, company analysis, and market questions.

**Focus mode** — A setting that constrains Perplexity's source set to a specific category. Available modes include Web, Academic, Writing, Video, Social, and Finance. Selecting the right Focus mode before searching improves source relevance.

**Follow-up question** — A subsequent query in the same thread that builds on previous context. Perplexity maintains conversation history within a thread, so follow-ups benefit from what has already been discussed.

**Grounding** — The process of anchoring an AI's output in verifiable, external information rather than relying solely on the model's training data. Perplexity grounds its responses by retrieving and citing web sources in real time. Grounding reduces hallucination.

**Hallucination** — When an AI model generates information that sounds plausible but is factually incorrect. This can include invented statistics, fabricated citations, or false claims stated with confidence.

**Image generation** — The ability to create new images from text descriptions. Available to Pro and Max subscribers in Perplexity.

**Large language model (LLM)** — An AI system trained on vast amounts of text data that can understand and generate human language. Perplexity uses multiple LLMs (from various providers) to power its responses.

**Model Council** — A Perplexity feature that sends your query to multiple AI models simultaneously and displays all responses side by side, allowing you to compare perspectives, identify consensus, and spot disagreements across models.

**OCR (Optical Character Recognition)** — Technology that converts images of text (such as scanned documents or photos of signs) into machine-readable text. Perplexity uses OCR capabilities when processing scanned PDFs and images containing text.

**Pages** — Perplexity's feature for generating structured, shareable research reports from your queries. Pages include organized sections, headings, inline citations, and a clean layout suitable for sharing with colleagues or publishing.

**Perplexity Computer** — An agentic AI tool launched in February 2026 for Max subscribers and enterprise users. Uses 19 different models to perform autonomous multi-step tasks. A "Personal Computer" companion device was announced as an always-on AI proxy.

**Perplexity Health** — A feature available to Pro and Max subscribers that connects to medical records from over 1 million providers for health-related research. Launched in early 2026.

**Perplexity Max** — The highest individual subscription tier at $200/month ($2,000/year). Provides access to the most capable models (such as o3-pro,

Claude Opus), unlimited research queries, and advanced features including Perplexity Computer.

**Perplexity Pro** – The standard paid subscription tier. Provides Pro Search credits, access to multiple AI models, image generation, and Deep Research.

**Pro Search** – An enhanced search mode that performs multi-step research and may ask clarifying questions before generating an answer. Uses more compute than standard search and is metered by credits on Pro plans.

**Prompt** – The text input you provide to an AI system. In Perplexity, your query is the prompt. Effective prompting – being specific, providing context, and specifying format – significantly improves response quality.

**Prompt engineering** – The practice of crafting inputs to AI systems in ways that produce better outputs. Techniques include role assignment, chain-of-thought prompting, constraint stacking, and negative instructions.

**RAG (Retrieval-Augmented Generation)** – A technique where an AI model retrieves relevant information from external sources (like the web) before generating a response. This is the core mechanism behind Perplexity's search-augmented answers.

**Role assignment** – A prompting technique where you tell the AI to respond from a specific perspective or expertise: "As a financial analyst..." or "As a pediatrician..."

**Social Focus** – A Focus mode that draws from community discussions on platforms like Reddit and forums. Useful for finding real-world opinions, user experiences, and practical troubleshooting advice. Previously called "Reddit" focus.

**Sonar** – The family of AI models powering Perplexity's API. Includes sonar (fast, standard), sonar-pro (higher quality), sonar-reasoning-pro (most capable reasoning), and sonar-deep-research (comprehensive multi-step investigation).

**sonar** – The base model in the Sonar API family. Fast and efficient, suitable for straightforward factual queries and high-volume applications.

**sonar-deep-research** — The Sonar API model designed for comprehensive, multi-step research investigations. Produces detailed reports but takes significantly longer than other models.

**sonar-pro** — A higher-quality Sonar API model that produces more detailed and nuanced responses than the base sonar model.

**sonar-reasoning-pro** — The most capable reasoning model in the Sonar API family, designed for complex analytical tasks that require step-by-step reasoning combined with web search.

**Space** — A persistent, named workspace in Perplexity that contains threads, custom instructions, uploaded files, and collaborators. Used for ongoing projects and team research.

**Streaming** — A method of delivering API responses where the text is sent incrementally as it is generated, rather than all at once after completion. Improves perceived performance in user-facing applications.

**Subscription model** — A business model where users pay a recurring fee for access to a service. As of early 2026, Perplexity has committed entirely to subscription revenue, having abandoned advertising. Tiers include Free, Pro, Max, Enterprise Pro, and Enterprise Max.

**Suggested follow-ups** — Questions Perplexity automatically generates after a response, based on what is likely to be useful given your query. They often surface angles or subtopics you had not considered.

**Thread** — A single conversation with Perplexity, consisting of your queries and the AI's responses. Threads maintain context, so follow-up questions can build on earlier exchanges.

**Thread library** — The collection of all your past Perplexity threads, accessible from the sidebar. You can search, pin, and delete threads from the library to keep your research organized.

**Token** — The basic unit of text processed by language models. A token is roughly four characters or three-quarters of a word in English. API pricing and context windows are measured in tokens.

**Valuation** — The estimated total market value of a private company, determined during fundraising rounds. Perplexity's valuation grew from approximately $520 million in January 2024 to roughly $20 billion by late 2025.

**Video Focus** — A Focus mode that searches video content including tutorials, lectures, product reviews, and demonstrations. Previously called "YouTube" focus.

**Visual search** — Using an image as a search query instead of text. Upload a photo and Perplexity identifies objects, reads text, or finds related information.

**Voice input** — The ability to speak your query aloud rather than typing it. Available in Perplexity's mobile apps via the microphone icon. Useful for long, context-rich questions that are tedious to type on a phone keyboard.

**Web Focus** — The default Focus mode. Performs a broad web search across all source types. Use this when your query does not fit neatly into another Focus category.

**Webhook** — A mechanism for one system to send real-time data to another when a specific event occurs. In the context of the Sonar API, webhooks can be used to receive notifications when asynchronous tasks (like deep research) complete.

**Writing Focus** — A Focus mode that shifts Perplexity away from web search and toward content generation. Use it when you want a draft, outline, or creative piece rather than a researched answer.

---

*Terms and definitions reflect the state of Perplexity and the AI industry as of early 2026. As the field evolves rapidly, some terms may gain new meanings or new terms may emerge.*

# Appendix E: What's New in 2025–2026

A timeline of major Perplexity AI developments for readers who want to understand how the platform reached its current state.

---

## 2024: The Breakout Year

**January 2024 — Funding and momentum.** Perplexity raised a $73.6 million Series B round led by IVP, with participation from NEA, Databricks, and prominent angel investors including Jeff Bezos. The round valued the company at approximately $520 million and signaled investor confidence in AI-native search.

**Q1 2024 — Rapid user growth.** Perplexity crossed 10 million monthly active users, establishing itself as the leading AI-native search alternative. The product found particular traction among researchers, developers, and knowledge workers who valued cited sources over raw chatbot output.

**March 2024 — Mobile app updates.** Major updates to the iOS and Android apps brought faster load times, improved voice input, and the ability to share content directly to Perplexity from other apps via the system share sheet.

**April 2024 — Series B1 extension.** An additional funding round brought valuation to approximately $1 billion, making Perplexity one of the fastest AI startups to reach unicorn status. The company had fewer than 50 employees at the time.

**Mid-2024 — Pages launch.** Perplexity introduced Pages, letting users turn research threads into structured, shareable, published web pages — a feature no competitor matched. Pages gave Perplexity a content-creation angle that distinguished it from both traditional search and pure chatbots.

**Mid-2024 — Spaces launch.** Collaborative research workspaces with custom instructions, file uploads, and team collaboration arrived, making Perplexity viable for team research. Spaces let users set persistent context so they did not have to re-explain their project with every query.

**September 2024 — Publisher controversies.** Several major publishers, including Forbes and Conde Nast, raised concerns about Perplexity summarizing their content without adequate attribution or compensation. This prompted an internal review and eventually led to the Comet Plus revenue-sharing model.

**Late 2024 — Advertising experiments.** Perplexity began testing sponsored follow-up questions and ad placements, drawing criticism from users who valued the ad-free experience. Revenue from ads proved minimal — roughly $20,000 of $34 million total 2024 revenue, confirming that the advertising model was not a natural fit for the product.

**November 2024 — Enterprise Pro launch.** Perplexity launched its enterprise offering with SSO, admin controls, data privacy guarantees, and per-seat pricing at $40/seat/month. Early enterprise customers included consulting firms, law practices, and research organizations.

**December 2024 — Series C.** A $500 million round valued Perplexity at approximately $9 billion, with participation from Institutional Venture Partners and other major investors. The funding was earmarked for infrastructure, hiring, and the development of what would become Comet Browser.

---

## 2025: Expansion and Evolution

**January 2025 — Sonar API.** Perplexity launched the Sonar model family as a developer API product, letting developers build search-powered applications on Perplexity's infrastructure. The initial lineup included sonar and sonar-pro models, with reasoning variants following shortly after. Pricing was competitive with existing search APIs, and the product found early traction among startups building research tools, customer support systems, and content platforms.

**Q1 2025 — Headcount and growth.** Perplexity's headcount grew past 200 employees, with heavy investment in infrastructure and model partnerships as user growth accelerated across all markets.

**Spring 2025 — Deep Research launch.** The first version of Deep Research arrived for Pro subscribers, capable of running multi-step investigations and producing structured text reports. Early reviews praised the depth of output but noted that queries could take several minutes to complete — a trade-off that would become a recurring theme as Perplexity pushed toward more thorough research modes.

**May 2025 — Mac desktop app.** Perplexity released a native Mac desktop application, giving users a dedicated window outside the browser with system-level keyboard shortcuts and faster access to search.

**July 2025 — Perplexity Max.** A new premium tier launched at $200/month ($2,000/year), offering access to the most capable models (o3-pro, Claude Opus 4/4.1 Thinking), unlimited research queries, and advanced features. Max targeted power users and professionals who needed the highest-quality output and were willing to pay for it.

**August 2025 — Ad sales head departs.** Signaling a strategic pivot away from advertising as a revenue model. The departure was widely interpreted as confirmation that Perplexity's future would be subscription-funded.

**October 2025 — Comet Browser.** Perplexity launched its own AI-powered web browser, Comet. Free to use, with a Comet Plus tier at $5/month that shares revenue with publishers whose content you browse — a novel approach to the publisher relationship problem that had dogged the company since mid-2024.

**October 2025 — Advertising wind-down.** Perplexity stopped accepting new advertisers, beginning the transition to a fully subscription-funded model.

**Late 2025 — Model expansion.** GPT-5 variants, Claude Sonnet 4.6, Gemini 2.5 Pro, and Grok 4 became available for Pro and Max users, giving subscribers access to the best models from across the industry within a single interface.

---

## 2026: The Subscription-Only Era

**February 2026 — Advertising abandoned.** Perplexity officially removed all advertising from the platform, committing entirely to subscription revenue. The company cited user trust as the primary motivation. Revenue target: $500M+ ARR from subscriptions alone.

**February 2026 — Perplexity Computer.** An agentic AI tool using 19 different models launched for Max subscribers and enterprise users. Perplexity

Computer can perform autonomous multi-step tasks, and a "Personal Computer" device was announced as an always-on AI proxy.

**February 2026 — Model Council.** A new feature letting users compare outputs from multiple LLMs simultaneously on the same query, helping researchers evaluate which model gives the best answer for their specific question.

**February 2026 — Perplexity Health.** Rolling out to Pro and Max subscribers, this feature connects to medical records from over 1 million providers for health-related research.

**March 2026 — Deep Research enhancements.** Deep Research expanded beyond text reports to generate presentations, spreadsheets, dashboards, and even websites from research prompts.

**March 2026 — Enterprise Max.** A new enterprise tier at $325/seat/month offering unlimited research queries, advanced models, and up to 10,000 files per user repository.

**Early 2026 — Focus mode evolution.** Focus modes updated: "YouTube" became "Video," "Reddit" became "Social," and a new "Finance" mode launched for SEC filings, corporate disclosures, and financial data. The "Wolfram" mode was retired as a standalone option.

**Early 2026 — Windows desktop app.** Perplexity's official Windows app became available through the Microsoft Store, joining the existing Mac desktop app.

---

## Growth Trajectory

| Metric | Early 2024 | Mid-2025 | Early 2026 |
|---|---|---|---|
| Monthly active users | ~10M | ~25M | ~30–45M |
| Daily active users | ~500K | ~1.5M | ~2M |
| Valuation | ~$1B | ~$9B | ~$18B |

| Metric | Early 2024 | Mid-2025 | Early 2026 |
|---|---|---|---|
| Annual revenue run rate | ~$34M (2024 total) | ~$148M ARR | ~$500M+ ARR target |

---

## What to Watch For

The pace of development at Perplexity shows no signs of slowing. Areas likely to see major developments:

- **Agentic capabilities:** Perplexity Computer expanding to handle more complex, multi-step autonomous tasks
- **Enterprise expansion:** Deeper integrations with corporate data sources and collaboration tools
- **Comet Browser:** Continued development as an AI-native browsing experience
- **Model diversity:** Additional model providers and specialized research models
- **Multimodal research:** Deeper integration of image, video, and audio analysis into research workflows
- **Publisher relationships:** Evolution of the Comet Plus revenue-sharing model

Stay current by checking Perplexity's blog at perplexity.ai/hub/blog and the resources listed in Appendix F.

# Appendix F: Resources and Further Reading

## Official Perplexity Resources

- **Perplexity AI:** perplexity.ai
- **Help Center:** perplexity.ai/help-center
- **Blog:** perplexity.ai/hub/blog
- **API Documentation:** docs.perplexity.ai
- **Comet Browser:** comet.perplexity.ai
- **Status Page:** status.perplexity.ai

## Staying Current

Perplexity evolves quickly. These resources help you stay current:

**Newsletters:** - Ben's Bites — Daily AI news digest - The Neuron — AI news for non-technical readers - Superhuman by Zain Kahn — AI productivity tips

**YouTube Channels:** - All About AI — Tutorials and feature walkthroughs - Matt Wolfe — AI tool reviews and news - The AI Advantage — Practical AI workflows

**Podcasts:** - Hard Fork (The New York Times) — Technology and AI news - The AI Daily Brief — Short daily AI updates - Latent Space — Technical but accessible AI discussions

## Books for Further Learning

**On AI and its implications:** - *Co-Intelligence* by Ethan Mollick — How to think about AI as a collaborator - *The Coming Wave* by Mustafa Suleyman — AI's broader societal impact

## Community and Learning

- **Reddit:** r/perplexity_ai — User discussions, tips, and discoveries

- **Discord:** Perplexity's official Discord community
- **X (formerly Twitter):** Follow @perplexity_ai for official updates
- **LinkedIn:** Follow Perplexity AI for professional perspectives

## For Developers

- **API Quickstart:** docs.perplexity.ai/docs/getting-started
- **Sonar Models:** docs.perplexity.ai/docs/models
- **API Pricing:** docs.perplexity.ai/docs/pricing

## Feedback and Updates

This book will be updated periodically to reflect changes in Perplexity's features and capabilities. For the latest edition and errata:

press.finnoybu.org

Found an error or have a suggestion? Contact:

press@finnoybu.org

www.ingramcontent.com/pod-product-compliance
Lightning Source LLC
LaVergne TN
LVHW060030210926
848481LV00013B/3826